Contents

* Not all these races are discussed within their usual 'season', but have been grouped together for convenience.

Foreword

I begin with a caveat. This is not the definitive history of Welsh fell running. It will not tell the story of the great and the good of the sport. It will not be a detailed account of who did what, or when they did it, or how long they took to do it.

Instead, it is one perspective on a precious sport: seasonal tales of Welsh mountain running revolving around the special races that grace all corners of our mountainous little country, and a celebration of the distinctive Welsh version of that sport.

In an inherently corporate world, with market forces dominating every aspect of life, where experience (and indeed life itself) is commoditised, running in the hills is also fundamentally political. Fell running is one of the last bastions of sporting purism, and it continues to hold out against those powerful market forces. That alone is a fact worth celebrating and exploring; and the Welsh version distils that ethos to its very essence – the races described pit runner against mountain, not for profit or social media boasting, but for the pleasure we derive from physical effort in spectacular landscapes.

The book is also about those landscapes, the environment we run in, its vulnerability and its significance. It is about the people – all the people – that participate in extraordinary races in extraordinary places in extraordinary conditions, wherever they finish in the field. And it is about the communities and the sports' relationship with those communities, which are often Welsh-speaking, sometimes fragile, and always distinctive.

Elite runners and exceptional achievements – of which there are many – will occasionally be mentioned, of course, as will the organisers, the progenitors, and the enthusiasts. But there will, inevitably, be omissions – for which I apologise in advance.

There is another caveat to get out of the way immediately. The very term 'fell running' is controversial in the Welsh context; it divides opinion. My own view is that it is slightly absurd to use the term 'fell' to refer to the Welsh hills. 'Fell' derives from the Norse 'fjell'; it is specific to the north of England, and to the Lake District in particular, a reflection of its ancient Scandinavian settlement. To transplant it to north Wales smacks of what some would call 'cultural cringe'. More to the point, it simultaneously manages to devalue the specific regional language and heritage of the Lake District by seeking to universalise it.

It is not a nationalistic response that makes me uncomfortable with the term 'fell running', in other words, more a case of being keenly aware that terms are specific, and if we lose reference to place we lose something important about our heritage. The Scots would never dream of calling their version of the sport 'fell running' (even though there actually are a few 'fells' in southern Scotland, Hart Fell near Moffatt for example: there are none in Wales.)

That said, I am aware that this debate divides opinion, and that the majority of Welsh mountain runners do prefer to use the term: it has long since taken root, and indeed it is used by the admirable governing body itself (the Welsh Fell Runners Association). So I will use the terms hill, mountain and fell randomly and interchangeably throughout the book – think of it as an imperfect solution to a tricky semantic conundrum.

What follows is an attempt to articulate one perspective on Welsh mountain running, woven around the narrative of the racing year and the geography of the Welsh landscape. The intention is to give a flavour of traditional fell (or mountain) races in all the varied upland corners of Wales, to tell the story of the sport both regionally and seasonally. Embedded within personal anecdote and material derived from a series of interviews with runners and race organisers is something of the flavour of each event, along with something of their history, which I hope taken together will shed some light on the overarching story of the sport in Wales. I have focused on the longer established races, and in that sense the book is only a snapshot – omissions are inevitable.

From the low but wild Preseli mountains in the south-west, legendary source of Stonehenge's Bluestones, to the green Clwydian hills of the north-east, and from the rolling grandeur of the Brecon Beacons to the jagged peaks of Eryri – every corner of our nation has its own distinctive version of the mountain landscape, and the book encompasses all of it.

That said, two more (final) caveats seem necessary: the first is that I live at the north-eastern fringe of Wales, so a small geographical bias may creep in from time to time, despite my best intentions. The second is that most fell races take place in summer, so there will inevitably be a preponderance of races that take place at that time. And one final point concerns measurements – the metric versus imperial debate has never been fully concluded in the world of fell running, despite the fact that the Ordnance Survey switched to metric in 1974 and the official body (the FRA) finally followed in 2016. As with the title of the sport itself, it still divides opinion. I have no intention of wading in, so will use metres and feet, miles and kilometres randomly and interchangeably.

Spring

Late March in the village of Llanuwchllyn, and the weather is bad. Nothing unusual for the time of year, perhaps, but if the wind is strong down here we all know what it will be like *up there* (as we insist on saying, knowing what's in store for us, reluctant to refer to anything too specific before the race). The village is archetypal north Wales, the very essence of the Bala hinterland despite its location near the busy main road that whisks tourists to Dolgellau and the coast. Its neat stone houses cluster around the hall and 'Tafarn yr Eryrod': on a day like this the architecture itself seems a completely organic part of the landscape, tasked with generating warmth and solidarity against the wild landscape that lies beyond.

Up there is the Aran ridge, close to 3000ft for two miles, and exposed to the full force of the north-westerly wind throughout. Down here, in the village hall, are about 100 runners, most of them well past the first flush of youth, most of them good-humoured wiry individuals experienced enough to extract the last bit of warmth from the hall's heaters before heading out into the horizontal sleet and the low-key start on the road. Virtually all are in vests and shorts, shivering, devoid of body fat, and apparently vulnerable – but today the race is declared compulsory 'full kit', meaning we all have small bum bags or tiny rucksacks containing waterproofs, map, compass and perhaps a hat and gloves. Maybe (whisper it) even a bit of chocolate, or a slice of cake.

This race, **Ras yr Aran**, is – even by the standards of Welsh mountain

Sunset from a wild camp on the Aran race route

running – uniquely 'hardcore'. I use the term advisedly. Unlike myriad commercial events that are usually no such thing, Ras yr Aran would never dream of describing itself as 'hardcore', or 'epic', or even 'challenging': indeed it would never dream of advertising itself at all – it is completely unheralded, known and loved only by a small band of connoisseurs. It costs £5 to enter: there are no medals, t-shirts or certificates. There are a few modest prizes for the winners, some bottles of beer, a box of chocolates. You might get a plastic cup of orange squash at the finish.

Out in the wilds of Meirionydd, far from centres of population, in many ways it typifies what I argue is a distinctively *Welsh* variety of mountain running. There is no real equivalent of this race in the Lake District, the Peak District, or even Scotland. By that I mean there is nothing else that goes quite so high, quite so early in the year; and not many races where you find yourself at such a remote highpoint, far from help, in March[1]. The top of Aran Fawddwy is just a shade under 3000ft, and a full five miles away from Llanuwchllyn.

As a result, the race tends to be memorable. From 76-year-old John Morris hypothermic in the village hall (having made sure he completed the race in good time, of course, before succumbing to the effects of the weather) to a group of top runners plunging down through the mist from Aran Benllyn into the wrong valley when it formed part of the Welsh Championships, interesting things happen on the Arans. According to Nicholas Bradley, the current organiser, not so long ago a local runner disappeared off to Rhyd-y-main when thick mist descended over Aran Benllyn, only to return on the back of a tractor a couple of hours later, just as people were beginning to wonder where he was.

It is one of the youngest races

covered in this book – it doesn't have the history of some of the longer established events that these chapters are intended to focus on. But it warrants its place for those reasons, its ambience and its unique position so early on the calendar. It was started in 2003 by Graeme Stringer and Tony Hodgson, local runners who joined Bradley and others to form Meirionydd Running Club after an amicable split from the Tywyn-based, and therefore rather distant, Bro Dysynni club in 2005. Meirionydd now makes an admirable attempt to stress its local identity, with its liberal use of the striking regional flag, often seen at a wide range of events in wild and remote locations. Three goats floating (or perhaps dancing) above a rising sun against a deep blue background; it might look like a psychedelic vision from Syd Barrett-era Pink Floyd, but it actually derives from a poetic description of the banner flown by the men of Meirioneth [sic] at the Battle of Agincourt.

As with most Welsh running clubs, Meirionydd makes a strenuous effort to promote athletics and mountain running in this sparsely populated corner of north Wales; this often goes unheralded, but it is important. There's no need to 'promote' fell running if you live in the Peak District, indeed many of the races over there are threatened by the sheer number of runners, but in the remoter parts of Wales such clubs play a big role in their communities and inculcate a love of our mountainous landscape that young runners will retain.

[1] Competitors on the Peak District's Wadsworth Trog, or our own Tarrenhendre race (both usually held in January) might dispute this – but they are both considerably lower in altitude and the general point, I think, stands.

As any climber or hillwalker will tell you, anything can occur in late March in the British mountains: it is the most unpredictable time of year by far. I've raced up Cumbria's High Street in the 'Lakes 42' to find its plateau-like summit a barely negotiable ice-sheet, almost a mini-glacier. I've baked in 24 degree heat on the rock climbs of the Moelwynion and been dehydrated in the Clwydian Hills, the landscape a dessicated shadow of its usual verdant self. I've climbed vertical ice in the Llanberis pass, and once came close to leading an American friend to his untimely death on the tiny, innocuous hill of Creigiau Gleision above Trefriw.

That was in the unusually frigid sub-zero March of 2013, in waist-deep snow drifts which had a thick, but eminently breakable crystallised ice crust which felt like shards of glass when you plunged through on every second stride. John, a colleague of mine at the time, came from New Jersey, had been a runner for 30 years and was experienced in the North American mountains, having 'walked alone for weeks and weeks in the Appalachians and Canada'.

He seemed well adapted to the core fell-running principles of self-sufficiency, so I had few concerns and certainly didn't intend to patronise or mollycoddle him. We met Mick Belshaw in Trefriw, and ran up to Crafnant, then Crimpiau, then along the skyline. John was fine across the tops, and seemed to be enjoying himself. Mick and I, the old mountain hands, monitored him subtly until just before the final descent back to the lake, when he slipped behind.

After a few minutes, I began to feel a slight sense of unease, and looked round just in time to see him on the skyline, half-heartedly raising his hand then keeling over onto the snowy ground. Broken ankle, I assumed, racing back up the slopes to help him out. He was unscathed, but badly hypothermic, unable to form words (an educated man, he was trying to say that he'd 'lost his equilibrium', not easy when the oxygen has left your brain). Between us, we forced some properly calorific food into him (a vegan, we discovered that he had been carrying only tomatoes and oatcakes), got him off the hill, into the car, cranked the heater on full blast, and by Colwyn Bay he had largely recovered (although he later developed septicaemia from the cuts on his shins, the ice crust had left his legs looking like he'd been run over by a tractor, and the wounds became infected).

It transpired that he had hidden his exhaustion from us as we traversed the exhausting drifts from Crimpiau to Creigiau Gleision, not wanting to lose face on our low Welsh hills.

On Ras yr Aran, I've seen fully frozen ponds on the summit ridge with icebergs in Llyn Pen Aran near the summit of Benllyn, been knocked over by ferocious 50 mile per hour gusts, and felt windchill so severe that it's given me a neck-clamping migraine – with the race shortened to just a bloodless hors d'oeuvre on Moel Ffenigl (still enough time for limbs to freeze and digits to numb). But I've also trotted up in glorious warm sunshine, sweating and desperate for water.

This time, this year, it's about average – cold, wet, windy and unpleasant, but not life-threatening. Nevertheless, on the top of Aran Fawddwy, in a force 9 gale and -20C windchill, no one can hear you scream.

The Aran race, therefore, seems a good place to start a seasonal guide to the rich traditions of long-established Welsh fell races. There is something about it that seems to typify the Welsh approach to the sport, which has a lack of commercialism at its very heart, a determined low-key minimalism woven into its fabric. That much is also still true of the Peak, Lakes and Scotland: all across Britain the basic ethos is zealously guarded. But I would argue that Welsh races often take it a step further – the fields are smaller, the venues more remote, the runners even more self-sufficient. In addition, our Welsh races are often centred around communities that represent the fragile essence of a distinctive culture. The resultant blend of languages, with runners drawn from a range of different backgrounds but all ultimately sympathetic to their surroundings (in the sense of both landscape and culture) adds an extra dimension and an extra appeal to Welsh mountain running which is often overlooked.

At one time, Ras yr Aran was centred on the Eagles pub (Tafarn yr Eryrod) in Llanuwchllyn; which has recently warped into a multipurpose focal point for this Welsh-speaking village, selling cabbages, milk and newspapers along with some excellent local beer. Now the race HQ is the village hall. It has, perhaps, lost a little something in the move from pub to hall, but it's a good second best which retains the community spirit and sense of place.

The race itself pelts through the village (blink and you'll miss it) for an entirely misleading few minutes of fast running; a flat, smooth tarmac sprint, before heading straight up to the low hill of Moel Ddu. The climbing starts the moment you turn off the tarmac, with steep fields leading to a cruel descent – an unwelcome break in the rhythm at

Ras yr Aran

this early point in the race – which leads to a large and invariably deep bog, the kind of thing that those ludicrous 'tough mudder' events have to artificially generate. There is nothing arbitrary about this one: it exists without hosepipes.

Then comes a series of rocky bluffs to the forepeak of Moel Ffenigl, after which the angle eases for a while (although the terrain underfoot remains awkward) until Aran Benllyn rears up ahead. This is a dreadful climb for the unprepared, and in bad weather the subsequent haul along the summit ridge can be very demanding. It is the length of this, continually exposed to the raking wind – generally blowing from the direction of Cader Idris in the West – that makes the race unusually vulnerable to the vagaries of the March weather.

'There's a great video of the little windmill, which sits in a field right at the bottom of the route, whirring round in a blizzard on race day,' says Nicholas Bradley. 'It does get the brunt of some pretty bad weather, even low down.' Everybody that organises a fell race has a difficult balancing act between the desire to allow people to run, to pit their skills against the weather and the environment, while remaining alert to the risks posed by the conditions. It is a fine line, and one that is taken seriously. 'We are very aware of the safety angle,' says Bradley. 'We don't take any decisions lightly. After the year in which numerous runners got lost, we did a big safety review looking at all the different incidents and analysing them.' They get it right. In the torrential rain and wind of the year described, the entire route was run except the very exposed and awkward summit cone, which is a steep pile of slippery scree at the best of times. True, John Morris got a touch of hypothermia, and Dawn Urquhart walked down in a mountain rescue thermal jacket – but I know both of them well, and neither of them complained, or felt the decision to be wrong. We all make that choice for ourselves.

Of course, there will always be a few who have different comfort boundaries, a different conception of what might be sensible. 'On one of those really cold years, it was absolutely bitter at the start, I can still feel the windchill when I think back,' says Flintshire runner Simon Edwards, who reckons he's done the race at least ten times. 'I was shivering in full kit, wondering what it might be like on top of Aran Fawddwy, and then I caught sight of a guy in a string vest, tiny skimpy shorts, carrying a miniature bumbag that looked more like a belt. I didn't recognise him, so I asked who he was. "Oh, that's the Yugoslav" [sic], came the reply. The "Yugoslav" apparently never carries much and doesn't feel the cold, no matter how appalling the weather might be. Later, when we'd finished, and I'd had a lovely hot shower in the hall and got changed into dry clothes, I wandered outside for a cup of coffee, and saw him in the river, stripped, chest-deep, cleaning the mud off in driving sleet, as if nothing could be more normal.'

And when it was really bad, in 2018, nobody complained when the race was shortened to Moel Ffenigl – there was no question of going up to the ridge given the severity of the windchill, let alone the marshalls staying up there for three hours in those conditions. The decision was correct and accepted – the organisers view vindicated.

'We all see the Aran race as completely different to Cader [Ras y Gader – in May],' says Bradley. 'Not just because of the time of year, but also because it's a low key race with a much smaller field, and the community chips in to help. We get a lot of help from local farmers, some have even carted lost runners back in their vehicles over the years.'

As an out-and-back course, at least you know exactly what you're in for on the descent, and there's always some prime Aran lamb to look forward to at the finish, along with a pint in the Eagles if you're lucky. Descents are where fell races are often won and lost: the differences between a timid descender and a naturally fast one are well-known and much-debated. For the lay person, there is something of a parallel with professional cycling. Watch the Tour de France in the Alps, for example, and no matter how well one of the lightweight riders climbs, they also have to be able to descend quickly, fluently and courageously if they are to win stages and races.

Once, on a beautiful midsummer's day, I camped on the race route, partly because this ridge offers views to east and west (for sunrise and sunset) but mainly because I felt it would be nice to spend some time here in good weather for a change. One of the many misconceptions about fell runners is that they are somehow immune to the natural beauty all around them, intent on rushing through the landscape. It's the kind of thing Alfred Wainwright might have said.

It is nonsense: we all love the landscape we are moving through, it's just that we are moving through more of it, more quickly. But it is nice to slow down once in a while, and I camped right on the route, just below Moel Ffenigl. It was June 2018, the middle of a desperately dry period across north Wales. A tiny trickle of peaty water lured me to a spot, and there I pitched: the drama of the race and the vagaries of the weather a distant but vivid memory as I watched the sun set over Snowdon.

1. Another Spring classic in the south: Pen Cerrig Calch (pic: Richard Cronin); 2. Marshalling on Ras yr Aran in full winter conditions (pic: Ashley Charlwood)

As Spring progresses, and warmer weather becomes tangible reality, the calendar fills up. After a winter racing on roads (perhaps) or (more likely) wading through bog and mist in a vain attempt to stay hill fit, the opportunity to race more frequently is welcome. In the north, most of the early season races are short blasts – like **Moel Wnion** above Bethesda, or the brutal **Pipe Dream**, which (as its name suggests) follows the route of the steep pipeline that drops down from Cwm Cowlyd high above. Its location always brings to mind R.S. Thomas's *Ancients of the World*, trying to dredge up the lines as some diversion from the hard panting agony of the climb through Coed Dolgarrog.

> The salmon lying in the depths of
>   Llyn Llifon
> Secretly as a thought in a dark mind
> Is not so old as the owl of Cwm
>   Cowlyd
> Who tells her sorrow nightly on the
>   wind.

After the race, sitting exhausted on the tiles of the Dolgarrog village hall, the remaining lines of the poem seem more pertinent, as I feel 'as old as the toad of Cors Fochno, who feels the cold skin sagging round his bones'.

In recent years, all the north's short races of late winter and early spring have been quietly joined by some longer events, some of which have a novel twist. So alongside the likes of the **Fron Four** near Penygroes and the **Llantysilio Mountain Race** above Llangollen now sits the **Clwydian Sheeptracks**, a fascinating addition to the calendar which sees the checkpoints disclosed to runners in advance by organiser John Heppenstall. They are free to reccie the route in their own time, finding the best lines, often by using those narrow tracks carved out by our ovine friends, making it something of a hybrid between a normal fell race and navigation-heavy events like mountain marathons (where the obscurely located checkpoints are revealed only

Llantysilio mountain race 2011 (pic: Al Tye)

at the start). In 2019, the Sheeptracks race formed part of the Welsh and north Wales championships and attracted a broad field of quality runners, some lured to embrace the concept from much further afield. It also coincided with a freak February heatwave of the kind that is becoming worryingly familiar, and there is not really any drinkable water in the Clwydians, which meant a desperate struggle for those foolish enough not to carry water in the second half of the race. I was one of those, limping up the road from Foel Fenlli to Bwlch Penbarras like a wounded animal, battered into submission by the unfamiliar heat.

Long-established races like **Moel Eilio** and Ras y Gader (both in May) have always had a devoted following. The latter, in particular, has become very popular in recent years whilst retaining its particular *genius loci*.

1. Autumn above Tal y Bont in the Conwy Valley; 2. Cwm Cowlyd; 3. Ras Moel Eilio (pic: Moel Eilio FB site)

Dolgellau is arguably the most distinctive and attractive of all Welsh towns and **Ras y Gader** is perhaps the race with the closest relationship to the community it begins from. It is paralleled, to an extent, by the Snowdon race, which is similarly entwined with Llanberis. Like Snowdon, Ras y Gader has gradually expanded from what was once a grass roots fell race to something rather more commercial. I first did it in the early noughties when you could enter on the day: now, it is online entries only, and those sell out in a few hours, rather like a painful 'type-two fun' version of Glastonbury. Despite that whiff of 'big commercial event', however, it retains its fundamental spirit of place and Eldon Square on race day is the closest thing to real atmosphere of any Welsh mountain race.

The nature of the challenge is so obvious, so compelling, that no mountain runner with blood in his or her veins can resist. The dark mass of Cader Idris looms above the town in much the same way that Snowdon rises above Llanberis, Ben Nevis above Fort William or the Matterhorn above Zermatt. Town and mountain are inextricably linked.

Eldon Square itself is the perfect place to start and finish a race to the top of one of the most legendary Welsh peaks, with its highly distinctive Meirionydd architecture – solid granite buildings huddling round the square, all built to resist the worst of the weather. A crowd builds as the start nears, a squadron of drummers play, an excited buzz takes hold as the runners begin to gather: it is all a far cry from the 'muddy field in the middle of nowhere' that often characterises Welsh fell race starts.

The race itself is something of a brute. Much of the start and finish, very unusually for a fell race, is on road: this has a tendency to lull runners into a false sense of security,

Ras y Gader (pic: Cambrian News)

despite the steepness. It seems... what's the word? Easy? Not quite that, but it does promote an urge to race, an urge which many later regret succumbing to as they flail through the cloying mud of the lakeside path, rubbery legs no longer able to obey the commands of the brain.

The race dates back to the early 80s. 'It was a totally barmy concept at first,' says Nicholas Bradley. 'Teams of three had to go part of the way up the mountain pushing a wheelbarrow.' Presumably, that seemed more sensible at the time than the idea of actually running unencumbered up and down the mountain. Nobody had really considered formalising it as a fell race until Don McCaffery and a group of local ambulance men organised it properly. Ever since, it's been run by what Bradley jokingly describes as 'a mafia-like, shadowy group called the committee'. And it has grown and grown, to the point that it sometimes sells out in a matter of hours.

'We deliberately call it a "mountain race" rather than a "fell race" because of the amount of tarmac, the length of the road section,' says Bradley, referring to the long initial haul that lures runners into the unwisest of fast starts. Like Snowdon, Ras y Gader has begun to attract a much broader field in recent years, with Garmin-equipped adventure runners and curious road runners now mingling with the hardcore fell runners. As Bradley points out, however, we are sometimes wrong to regard those new to traditional mountain running as more vulnerable to the elements, as it is often the most experienced fell runners who play fast and loose with the kit requirements. 'We had a girl break her leg near the summit a few years ago. She overbalanced and would have been pretty cold by the time the helicopter arrived, even though it was a nice day – that's what it's like high up, of course. But she had the right kit, she'd packed more than we ask for, and that helped her a lot.'

Ras y Gader is another of those

blue-riband Welsh events boasting a long-standing record time, in this case Colin Donnelly's 1.21.18 recorded in 1996. Lloyd Taggart came within seconds of breaking this in foul weather in 2011, but apparently had to stop to tie his laces on the descent. Mary Wilkinson's impressive female record of 1.33.58, set in 2006, will also take some beating.

I first did Ras y Gader in 2005 as a relative neophyte with a lingering spare tyre. That year, the race coincided with the kind of early summer weather front that occasionally wreaks havoc higher up on these Westerly coastal peaks. As a result, it was shortened: turned back at the flat plain of Rhiw Gwredydd well before the climb up the rocky slopes of the main peak.

This does happen from time to time at fell races, and generally provokes much wailing and gnashing of teeth among competitors. For race organisers, it is a tricky decision. On the one hand, the desire of entrants to run whatever the weather, and the ethos of self-sufficiency in the mountains, is a fundamental tenet of the sport. On the other, however, the safety and comfort of race marshalls, who may spend hours checking numbers in remote parts of the Welsh mountains, often on rain-lashed high summits, is equally important, as are basic safety concerns for the runners themselves. Tales abound of runners so enraged by cancellations that they run the route anyway – Ben Nevis in 1980 is a famous example, the only time in its long history that the elements forced the organisers to abandon the race. A small group ran to the top anyway, in what must have been genuinely appalling conditions.[2]

Regardless of the rights and wrongs of race shortening (or, worse still, cancellations) one thing is certain: if you are unfortunate enough to experience one, you'll consider it unfinished business and will be back for the full dose next time. So it was with Cader: I was back the next year, and was overconfident. In a previous existence, in the early 1990s, I lived in a dilapidated builder's portakabin above Penrhyncoch in the Aberystwyth hinterland: no toilet, no running water, appalling food. Cader Idris, as our 'local' hill, was a frequent destination for the school groups booked into the cut-price field studies centre I worked in. Every week, a reluctant group of teenagers from the flatlands of Hampshire or Essex would be cajoled and coaxed up the hill, continually asking 'are we nearly there' until becoming disillusioned with my stock (and entirely fictitious) 'ten minutes' reply.

So I set off too fast, familiarity breeding contempt, relishing the climb, relishing the descent, but underestimating the length of the return. On reaching the road high above Dolgellau, where any normal, well-adjusted Cader Idris hillwalker parks, the race route takes a cruel detour to contour round the shores of Llyn Gwernan. This has a tendency towards bogginess and is notoriously energy sapping. The transition from galloping downward pelt on the descent to flailing through a flat bog with jelly legs and an aching back is the crux of Ras y Gader and has caught many runners out over the years. I was no exception, limping back down the tarmac to Eldon Square; a sad, shrivelled husk of my former self. It got considerably worse as I repeatedly vomited on the journey home, my still untrained stomach violently rejecting the sandwiches and cakes offered by the wonderful support team in the town hall.

I'd persuaded my old friend Dave Lynan to come down from Liverpool for the day. His white Penny Lane Striders vest was speckled with dark brown manure, but he was in much better shape than me. With two tiny children, the frequent vomiting stops (both within and outside the car) all the way home tested the patience of my companions to breaking point. It took years before Dave joined me again on a fell race, and my wife Kate and the kids began their long journey from acceptance, through resigned tolerance, to complete rejection of my extra-curricular activities.

These kind of salutary experiences are common. You emerge a little wiser, with a better-trained stomach, and a tad more cautious.

[2] The cultural, and attitudinal, differences between fell and road running were perfectly illustrated one weekend in February 2020. Storm Denis blew in just in time for the **Conwy Mountain fell race**. This event, first run in 2017, makes the most of the little hills above the town and there was no question of it being called off or curtailed, despite the 65mph gusts scouring the summits. It gave a memorable battle into a vicious headwind on Allt Wen: nobody complained, and much fun was had. Next day, the wind had dropped considerably, no more than 20mph, and the rain finally stopped. But the Wrexham half marathon, for which I also had a place, had already been cancelled.

Conwy Mountain race

In the south of Wales, Spring comes that tiny bit earlier, or so it seems to me. The Brecon Beacons, the Black Mountains and the hidden mountains of the south-west have fewer races than the north – but it is only marginal, and come spring there is plenty of action, from steep and explosive races like **Cribyn** and **Pen Cerrig Calch** through to slightly longer and more serious events like the **Tour of Torpantau** (on which I and many others got lost in freezing mist in 2013 – my feeble excuse, as we drowned our sorrows and defrosted in Pencelli's Royal Oak, was that I followed two local Mynydd Du runners, only realising that we were heading east, away from the first checkpoint, when it was too late and the clag was so thick we could barely read our compasses).

Mynydd Troed, such a notable feature of the south Wales upland landscape, also features in a long-established late Spring race (recently reconfigured and relaunched as the **Cwmdu fell race**). This event coincided with an appalling day of rain and wind in 2012, which saw paths pouring with mud, water and floating rocks, and runners knocked down like skittles in the intense cross-wind. My billowing waterproof trousers acted as impromptu parapentes at one point, blowing me uphill in a blissful reversal of the usual headwind battling that renders such conditions physically draining. At the start, the marshalls were keen to impress on us that the route had been shortened, that it was absolutely critical to turn right at one crucial junction, not left. So keen were they to convey this fact that they shouted out the question to cement the route change in our oxygen-deprived runners' brains. 'Which way do you turn?', they barked: 'Right!', we all yelled back in unison. At the junction, I turned left ...

Later, as we dried off in Pengenffordd above Talgarth, some alarming news filtered through:

'John's in trouble'. We rushed out of the pub to find 70-year-old John Morris being helped down from the finish in an advanced state of hypothermia. His condition was genuinely concerning (even though he had put in his usual superb performance on the race itself), his clothes were removed by a gaggle of female helpers in front of the pub fire, an ambulance was called, and we spent the rest of the day at the Nevill Hall hospital in Abergavenny. John had a whale of a time, making friends with several nurses, and – once released – singing happily in the back of the car all the way home.

One of the longest established events in the south is the point-to-point

1. Cwmdu fell race (pic: Richard Cronin);
2. Cwmdu race

Llanbedr-Blaenafon which, for a visiting north Walian, seems to represent the very essence of south Wales in one memorable journey. It is the ultimate blend of Black Mountains beauty and Valleys grit. With its all-you-can-eat spread in the rugby club after the race, and its 'ad hoc' transport arrangements, it also gets close to expressing the unassuming essence of the sport in Wales. I first ran it in 2011, and still retain the memory of a perfect early Spring day, the most wonderful time of year in the Welsh countryside, when the landscape sparkles and the hills glisten, etched in perfect clarity against a deep blue sky.

I was recovering from injury at the time, a serious knee problem that had put me out of action for three long winter months, so just being able to run was a relief: the linear nature of the course an ideal motivator for very obvious reasons (dropping out would be inconvenient, embarrassing and potentially expensive).

It is now organised by international mountain runner and former British champion Ruth Pickvance, although the man responsible for the race's inception was Gareth Buffett, a Lake District doctor who had enjoyed fell running in the place where the sport originated. In the Lakes, the classics are long-

Llanbedr-Blaenafon race: Cresting the Blorenge (pic: Al Tye)

established, and essential 'ticks' for any serious fell runner – Ennerdale, Wasdale, Borrowdale – all elegant horseshoes around beautiful valleys. Gareth moved to south Wales in the late 70s but was surprised to find a lack of races over what had become his new local hills – they seemed obvious candidates for similar events to those in the Lakes, in fact they are more suitable in some respects, green, grassy and eminently 'runnable'.

Phil Davidson was a pastor who had, by coincidence, also moved to the area from the Lakes. Inevitably, the two eventually bumped into each other on one of their long runs over the Black Mountains. 'There just wasn't much around here at the time, despite all the mountains and obvious routes,' says Gareth. 'Phil and I did a few more runs together and between us we decided to get something organised.' The result was Llanbedr-Blaenafon, which Gareth – after rooting through his records – reckons

started in 1979, making it one of the oldest fell races in Wales. I asked about the distinctive point-to-point nature of the course, as I have always been curious about it. 'Well, as far as I remember the linear course was Phil's idea,' says Gareth. 'I actually wanted to work out a horseshoe, like all the best Cumbrian races'.

From the pretty village of Llanbedr, hidden away down twisting lanes which our group of north Wales raiders had reached 'ad hoc' by packing into one tiny Toyota, the race heads down a cobbled track before surprisingly runnable contouring paths lead gradually to the breezy top of Crug Mawr. At this point, the views north over the Black Mountains open out, and in 2012 a light mist draping the higher hills began to dissipate as we climbed, giving way to perfect clarity and expansive views. A long descent into Cwm Beusych follows, before the crossing of Grwyne Fawr to more gently rising paths which lead to a fine ridge up to the celebrated Sugar

Loaf, a well-known Gwent landmark.

Then come multiple opportunities to get lost on the descent into St Mary's Vale, before even trickier 'urban navigation' through the edge of Abergavenny, over the Usk, to a sidelane leading up to water and snacks at Llanfoist.

This road section was really tough given the recent injury problem that had prevented me from training, and I knew I needed to eat something before the final brutal slog up the Blorenge. I downed a gel saved from a famous cycle sportive, the 100 mile Cheshire Cat, that I'd done the week before (like many injured runners, I had switched to cycling during my injury, using it as a means of staying fit, and sane). I began to feel ill almost immediately, just managing to maintain a steady chug up this famously steep hill. After leaving the woods, the path gets steeper and steeper until most runners are on all fours for the final section, emulating a well-adapted quadruped, an Alpine chamois perhaps. There are, literally, hand and foot holds up this climb: they have been worn into the hard-packed mud by multiple thousands of exhausted limbs. Eventually, this appalling steepness dissipates as the race route gains the peaty plateau summit of the Blorenge, after which it's still a fair distance to the finish through the maze of confusing terraced streets that mark the entry into south Walian mining territory. The rugby club is there, hidden away in Upper Blaenafon, but after 14 miles, with an addled brain starved of oxygen, it's not easy to find. Since then I've heard numerous tales from my fellow north Walians, unfamiliar with the area, running round the terraced streets of upper Blaenafon in a blind panic, desperately looking for the rugby posts.

The sub-two hour record recorded by James McQueen in 1999 has stood for a very long time (although not as long as Menna Angharad's astonishing female record of 2.19, set in 1996). Gareth Buffett's memory is that McQueen's time derived from a year in which the race formed part of the British Championships (this is a four-race series, which changes every year and usually includes one event in each 'home nation').

'On the year the record was broken the top runners cheated, although only very slightly, by taking a little short-cut up Crug Mawr, so the times are not strictly comparable,' says Buffett, tongue firmly in cheek. They got to the tops of the three peaks, though, and the standard of competition in any British championship race is always pretty extraordinary: no quarter is given. Andy Darby, a local farmer, is probably the most prolific all-time winner of the race, with 'four or five victories in the early years', according to Buffett.

Snorkel and flippers are not on the kit list for **Ras Beca**, but they might as well be. This corner of the Preseli hills is semi-aquatic at the best of times and the race revels in its landscape, plunging (literally) into it from the very start. It is a long journey from my home in the north-eastern borderlands to the opposite corner of the country, so I've only done it once, when chasing the Welsh Championships in 2011. At the time, I wrote that the race is 'perhaps better suited to amphibians and other aquatic creatures than normal primates'. Hurtling waist-deep into icy water is a regular feature; indeed the finish is deliberately set up for the amusement of spectators, who can arrange themselves in the most advantageous position to indulge in a spot of schadenfreude when runners fall into the unseen and impossible-to-judge depths of the bog. This is not a commercial 'obstacle race', though: this is a real bog, not an artificial construction, and that is genuine Pembrokeshire peat that you'll be scraping of your calves for days.

Unusually for a fell race, it is taped towards the finish along a fairly strict slalom route – but this is not so much a navigational aid, more a way of ensuring the runners cannot avoid the sludge so they can provide maximum entertainment for the hardy locals who come out to watch. The twists and turns maximise the difficulty of the terrain. And, again, unlike most fell races, there are real spectators here – it is a big community event, with a well-attended junior race, Mochyn Du, lending it a multi-generational feel that remains quite rare.

Ras Beca

DIWEDD

Start and finish of Ras Beca

We camped in a tranquil spot below the hills in Blaenffos, notable for me because it was the last time I was ever allowed to incorporate a family weekend camping into an important race. The campsite had an eco-toilet, the archetypal plunge into a dry compost pit, and my wife Kate was not happy. Later that evening, shivering outside the tent on our decrepit deck chairs in down jackets, I offered her a bottle of 'Old Speckled Hen' by way of placation. She looked me straight in the eye, unsmiling, and said: 'we are never doing this again'. She was true to her word: we never did. Instead, I've spent the intervening years pioneering the car bivouac and testing my flimsy 700 gram mountain marathon tent to solo destruction.

Ras Beca starts in the middle of nowhere and negotiates a neck-deep bog after a few hundred metres of flat-out sprint. This sets the tone: bog and tussocks across an empty moor heading for the mercifully dry(ish) slopes of Carn Goedog. Local knowledge helps for this initial section, so I inevitably lost ground before clawing a bit back as we ran across the main Preseli ridge to Mynydd Bach and along the side of Foel Feddau. Then comes the bog of Waun Brwynant. This is so deep and hard to run through that almost all competitors suffer at least one headlong fall (I later discovered I'd bruised my armpit, a novel injury). Then comes a manic finish, which involves negotiating the previously mentioned taped-off maze through a giant bog with numerous stretches of waist-deep open water (this bit, which always provides amusement for spectators, was apparently filmed by drone in 2017 – a sign of things to come, perhaps).

The race was first run in 1977, and commemorates the celebrated 'Rebecca Riots' when farm workers radicalised by a wide range of iniquities smashed the hated local toll gates whilst disguised as women. It's the best regional reference of all, an overtly political nod to the past and a celebration of a vitally important slice of Welsh history. The link is maintained throughout, with the winners using a ceremonial axe to destroy a reconstruction of a toll gate. It's hard to imagine a better expression of place, or a more effective illustration of the link between race and locality, embedded as it is within its community and its landscape.

Given that, it seems appropriate that the race record is one of the longest standing of all Welsh fell races, 32 minutes and 5 seconds, set by St Dogmaels triathlete Aled Rees way back in 1995. There have been a few 'dry years' since then (the term being highly relative in this part of the world) in which conditions seemed ripe for the record to be broken, but nobody has got anywhere near to it. Having only done it once, I have no idea what might be considered 'dry', but the fact that I got my neck and ears wet suggests that it wasn't in 2011.

For kinder terrain underfoot, the green hills of north-east Wales always provide 'entry level' opportunities for those trying to make the transition from road to hill. The **Moel y Gamelin** fell race is a case in point, although as a 'medium' race it often takes outsiders by surprise – the hills above Llangollen look so beautifully inviting and gentle[3] from the touristy town that it comes as something of a shock to find steep gradients and awkward scree along the main ridge line. A visiting Gwent runner described the final climb as 'an utter bastard' to me after finishing the race on one of the years that it formed part of the Welsh Championships. It starts and finishes at the famous bikers' café of the Ponderosa at the top of the Horseshoe Pass; often a source of some friction given the sheer numbers that come up here in summer (the race takes place in June).

The 2018 race was typical. At the start, just above the Ponderosa, the weather was baking: it often is down here on the western slopes in midsummer, far from water, far from any kind of breeze. You fry, you cook; it always seems to be the hottest race of all (not every year, of course – in 2013 it took place in constant rain, persistent clag and a howling gale, which turned into a helpful tailwind for the dreadful final climb back over the main peak of Moel y Gamelin).

It's a local race for me, so I've done it at lot, at least 10 times, making it hard to distinguish between them. So memories of the race tend to be generic and fragmentary, although often characterised by heat, dehydration and sunburn. It is long enough to make water essential – but dry enough to make stream-dipping virtually impossible (drinking from streams quickly and efficiently is an essential skill for all fell runners – suspicion of which generally indicates a neophyte, or someone who will just be too fastidious and therefore unsuited to the task in hand).

The Horseshoe Pass is an

unusually high place to start a fell race, which means that the first climb – up Moel y Faen – is, in relative terms, quick and easy. It is over within a matter of minutes, which – as with the tarmac on the Cader race – lulls runners into a false sense of security. The ridge then undulates, quite dramatically, dipping like a rollercoaster over Moel y Gamelin and Moel Morfydd before heading out to the wild moorland above the village of Carrog in the Dee Valley. This region was hit by a terrible heathfire at the height of the summer drought in 2018. It led to some races being cancelled, as the flames lurked under the heather for days on end, irrupting then dying in cycles in the dry weather. Now, the landscape is scorched, a black shadow of its former self. It will recover eventually, but in the meantime the race has a desolate, apocalyptic character until the far end is reached, after which it becomes more like a gigantic cross-country race, with fast running out to the west. Given the time of year, this is where things get tough, dehydration kicking in until a tiny road and wonderful marshals (the race is organised by Charles Ashley and his Wrexham team-mates) provide water and the possibility of momentary relief.

The race climaxes in a hellish climb back up to the summit of Moel y Gamelin, using the celebrated 'Conquering Hero' track, which ultimately leads to the village of Llantysilio in the beautiful upper Dee valley: its unusual name is because it was named after a pub, long since closed.

[3] Indeed, one of them is called 'Velvet Hill', which I have always presumed to be a reference to its alluring softness when seen from the banks of the Dee.

There is one little race up here in the Clwydian Hills that has put more road runners off the transition to the hills than any other: and it happens to be the only race I organise myself. It takes place a little later in summer, usually on the Wednesday evening closest to the solstice: **Hotfoot up Famau**. A mere 3.5 miles in length, just a tad more than a standard 5k Parkrun, it has often lured unsuspecting road runners onto its challenging terrain. Richard Bolton, a Warrington-based fell runner and distance specialist, told me that it still has legendary status among the road runners of the town, after they innocently chose to include it as part of their summer 'trail running' series. After plunging through neck deep ferns to the Vale of Clwyd, the realisation dawns: this is emphatically not a trail race – nor does it simply dash to the summit and back, as its name suggests.

The race was founded by Martin Cortvriend, who did a great deal to inculcate a real fell running culture into the Clwydian hills. Martin launched a whole series of races after moving to an isolated farmhouse above Llangynhafal, an enviable position for a keen runner to find himself in, just below the main Clwydian ridge with its wonderful sweeping descents and sharp climbs. Some of the races were relaunches of older, established events, like the **Llangynhafal Loop** (which was later taken over by Huw Lewis of Mynydd Isa, and is now held in Spring) while others came from Martin's own feverish imagination[4]. Hotfoot was one of those.

I tend to describe it to aspirants as 'the least logical possible way to the summit of Moel Famau', as it almost immediately plunges *downhill* from the start at Bwlch Penbarras. This is counter-intuitive and therefore psychologically damaging, and gives way to a battle through neck-deep

Moel Famau (pic: Jeremy Randell)

ferns before a vicious climb to the ancient hillfort of Moel y Gaer, with runners struggling to avoid oxygen debt, or what my wife still rather quaintly describes as 'getting puffed out' (any 70s schoolchild will recognise this phrase).

This is the essence of the short fell race experience. Indeed, in any form of running, the distance is a largely irrelevant guide to how 'hard' the race might be. What is relevant is the physical battle to eke out energy resources, to adapt to wildly spiking heartrates and wildly different terrain. The unusually early descent means that there is inevitably a temptation to sprint downhill, to fly like the wind, to over-stride. Equally inevitably, by the time the route flattens out as it reaches the edge of the Vale of Clwyd, the entire field has legs full of lactic acid, but there is no recovery time before a 300ft climb up a tiny path that threads its way through heather and gorse to the top of Moel y Gaer. After a brief respite along a short ridge, perhaps two minutes of gentler running, it plunges down again, through steep bracken-clad slopes down to the base of Nant y Ne.

Next comes the legendary 'gully', known and feared by all fell runners who have visited these parts. A complete contrast to the usual verdant softness of the Clwydians, it is a rocky gash dropping down from the summit that nobody in their right mind would think of incorporating into a Moel Famau visit. The multiple thousands of Liverpudlians and other day-trippers that trudge up the hill every year would never even suspect its existence, hidden away, unseen, high above Llanbedr Dyffryn Clwyd.

Back in 2007, Martin Cortvriend lured the British fell running relays to Llangynhafal. This was, I think, the first time (and still the only time) that this major event has taken place in the Clwydian Hills. After completing the long pairs leg, I marshalled at the top of the gully, keen to see whether the top runners ran the whole way. Answer: yes, but only a few. In the summer of 2019, nobody did, as torrential rain left the gully resembling a mini-Niagara, torrents of white water pouring over the boulders.

Moel Famau remains the focus of multiple races up in the north-east, most of which attract big fields, which is a reflection of the Clwydians' geographical location near the urban centres of north-west England. Some English clubs near the border, like Helsby, Pensby and Tattenhall, have a long fell running tradition, and their colourful vests are a constant feature of races across those green hills. The longest established is arguably still the blue riband event in these parts, the **Cilcain Mountain Race**, which has been a pivotal part of the village show held in Flintshire's prettiest village every August Bank Holiday. It shares centre stage with dog races, parachuting teddy competitions (from the church spire) and multiple cake baking competitions. For many people, over many years, it has been their first experience of a genuine fell race – and it's an obvious choice, with its steep climb but relatively kind descent, and its foolproof navigation. It was my first fell race too, in 2003, and I've done it every year since (almost).

There is a special atmosphere at the summer evening races across the Clwydians. The weather is usually nice (not always: in 2019 my Hotfoot up Famau took place on a day of near-constant rain, our results sheets pulped as Jeremy Randell and Huw Lewis valiantly struggled to take the runners' numbers), and the lure of a pleasant country pub is never far away. Indeed, the **Druid fell race** takes its name from the pub of the same name in Llanferres, and **Up the Beast** finishes at the Miner's Arms in Maeshafn, a nod to the heritage of this beautiful landscape. The Beast was launched by local legend John Morris, the ominous title of the race a

reference to the local nickname for the steep climb through little crags to the limestone pavement on top of Bryn Alyn. The route has changed a bit over the years, and we once had the amusing spectacle of half the field going the wrong way through the dense woodland above the Big Covert quarry. This led to a unique finishing line scene, with 50% of the runners crossing in one direction, and the other 50% running towards them from the opposite.

John's special brand of humour led to him describing the event as a 'trail race' in the early years, an epithet vigorously disputed by entrants as they clambered up vertical limestone walls, using hands as well as feet, in their efforts to reach the top.

[4] One of the first ever was the Foel Fenlli race in 2002 or 2003 (its much-altered course is now taken by the Druid race). This left the infamous Clwyd Gate restaurant, now a derelict eyesore at the highpoint of the Ruthin-Mold road. It was one of my first ever fell races, and I have a vivid memory of vomiting over the Foel Fenlli cairn, unprepared as I was for the double ascent. I remember thinking 'surely once is enough' as I decorated the stones.

1. Beast race route on New Year's Day; 2. Beast race route; 3. Colomendy route up Moel Famau on a winter evening

In the Welsh mountain running heartland further west, at the height of summer, one race dominates: **Snowdon**.

Ask most fell runners about **Ras yr Wyddfa** and the word you will hear used most frequently is 'carnage'. Over-dramatic perhaps, but it goes some way to describing the scenes in the medical tent, which often resembles a wartime field hospital – broken bones, bruises, and blood. In some respects the most hazardous race on the Welsh mountain running calendar, it is also by some margin the most prestigious. It is the only race on which you might be filmed, and rub shoulders with Kenyans; and you will certainly rub shoulders with Italians – given the links between Llanberis (and local club Eryri Harriers) and Morbegno, which nestles at the base of the Valtellina on the edge of the Italian Alps. Ras yr Wyddfa is also the venue for the home international championships, so Irish, English and Scottish vests mingle with the cream of Welsh mountain running talent.

Vic Belshaw, like many others, cites his first experience of the Snowdon race as being the spark that lit his running fuse, the point of departure for decades of fell races. Belshaw is a classic example of a 'climber turned runner'. There are, essentially, two routes into mountain running and most fell runners fit into one or other of the categories. The first is made up of road runners who get bored and want to broaden their horizons; the second is made up of climbers (or hill-walkers, or other mountain enthusiasts) who, for whatever reason, are trying something different but related. Sometimes, they just want to go faster through the landscape, often for quite logical reasons.

In my case, I was a hillwalker and climber (of very modest ability) who had loved being in the mountains since my teenage years, and needed to

Above Pen y Gwryd looking towards Yr Wyddfa

be amongst them regularly. However, by the turn of the millennium, with small children and limited time, I needed to adapt, to get among them more quickly if I was going to continue to get my 'mountain fix'. The solution was obvious: go faster.

I had already revived my running career, in 1998, after an Alpine trip with my long-term climbing partner Tim Holt that summer. We had always been equally matched physically and had started climbing together in the late 80s from our Vale of Clwyd homes. Since then, however, Tim had become a teacher in the Lake District, whilst I – in stark contrast – was a business journalist in London. My palms had grown soft, a spare tyre was developing around my midriff, and a new chin was visible. We set our sights on the Nadelhorn above Saas Fee in Switzerland, after being beaten down from the remote Konkordia hut in dreadful weather.

The Nadelhorn is a relatively straightforward peak by its north-east ridge, but I was suffering like a dog in the thin air as we approached its 4327m summit. I detected, to my horror, that Tim was dragging me up, as if I was indeed an ageing poodle on a lead. Never again, I thought, and started pounding the streets of Ealing and Acton in West London as soon as I returned home. By 2001, I'd run my first London marathon and by 2003, my first fell race. Then, in 2005, we went to the north-west Highlands with young children. I'd been running for eight years and had done quite a few fell races by then, but I was still far too slow and still carrying a bit too much timber around the waist. I headed up Slioch from Kinlochewe, but the bedraggled figure that limped back to our cottage several hours late did not endear himself to his family as the evening meal congealed on the plate. It all took too long, and so did the short trip round the peaks of Beinn Alligin two days later. It was time, in short, to take it a bit more seriously.

For Belshaw, the same Damascene conversion was more precise, and remains crystallised in his memory: 'I remember seeing the Italians flying up Snowdon, and then the top boys from the Lakes descending with white flecks spraying everywhere – it looked like they were foaming at the mouth. I thought, "wow, this is a sport for me". It fitted very nicely into my routine at the time – I was living in north Anglesey, still a keen climber, but not always able to get out as often as I would have liked. Running was the answer, and one thing led to another.'

The Snowdon race often attracts road runners and those looking for an obvious 'challenge'. As such, it has become rather too commercial in recent years for many traditionalists – although in reality that commercialisation is an understandable, perhaps inevitable response to the demand for places and the contemporary reality that these sorts of high-profile events are always likely to draw a big field of entrants from all sorts of backgrounds.

Whatever your thoughts on the topic, it (like the Ben Nevis race, its closest equivalent) remains pretty special, and it also has the kudos of boasting one of the oldest, and most remarkable, of all race records – Kenny Stuart's 1 hour, 2 minutes and 29 seconds, a 'wings on feet' time that evades comprehension, set way back in 1985 (Carol Greenwood's female record of 1.12 is just an impressive and almost as old, having stood since 1993). Since then, it has been won by dozens of illustrious athletes on that hallowed route up from Llanberis – from five times world mountain running champion Marco de Gasperi, to English fell running legend Ian Holmes, to top Manchester athlete Andi Jones; along with Scottish runners like Robbie Simpson, Murray Strain and Angela Mudge, and Wales' own Tim Davies, British fell running champion in 2010. In 2018, Bronwen Jenkinson became the first Welsh winner of the women's race since Angela Carson in 1989.

1. Pen y Fan (pic: Crispin Flower);
2. Ras y Cnicht (pic: ClicClic)

For the hardcore put off by Snowdon's modern commercial incarnation, there are myriad alternatives because the months of June, July and August represent the peak of the fell running season. **Moel Hebog** is often described as a 'mini-Ben Nevis': the implication being that it resembles that famous race up Scotland's highest peak, as an out-and-back sprint through some very

technical terrain, rocky and awkward throughout and a nightmare for those unfamiliar with it. Having done both, I would say it is a fair comparison, albeit around half the length. Further south, **Pen y Fan** is another of those races with very old record times for both men and women – so old, in fact, that £100 is offered for anybody that can break either of them (if you fancy your chances, the target is Keith Anderson's 30.00 set in 1992, and Calder/Crofts joint record of 38.15, also set in the early 90s).

In the Clwydian Hills, a series of midweek evening races fully embrace the non-commercial ethos, and Mike Blake's summer Tuesday series further west takes that a step further, with each a mere £2 to enter. **Moel Siabod** is another long-established race that attracts runners from further afield, lured by that mountain's fame and shapely profile. It is held in conjunction with the Capel Curig village show, echoing a phenomenon that remains a little more common in the Lake District, bringing community, mountain and athlete together in an appealing blend. Siabod is a classic 'up-and-down', with the sub-hour return target an attractive and realistic aim for quicker runners. **Ras Cnicht** is even quicker: a short but immensely steep blast up the rocky 'Welsh Matterhorn' from the village of Croesor, the home of the late Bob Owen, a legendary working class autodidact who built up an immense library of books. Cnicht allows for the ultimate post-race treat, a soak in the icy waters of the slate pool in the village which is filled by a diverted mountain stream. This is helpful for damaged quadriceps, because the descent down its rocky slopes is unusually technical and demanding, taking in an open chimney of rock near the summit.

Moving a long way south to Bedwas, near Caerphilly, **Guto Nyth Brân** is a low-key commemoration of the local link with that most famous of all Welsh runners (he is also celebrated by the popular Nos Galan 5k road race held every New Year's Eve around the streets of Mountain Ash, which always features a mystery Welsh sporting hero as starter).

Legend has it that Guto died, aged 37, after a 12 mile race between Newport and Bedwas, collapsing after

a particularly brutal final uphill sprint. It is a legend to chill the heart of the average fell runner, as 37 would be considered the young side of prime for most of us (peak performances often tend to come between the ages of 38 and 42, although there are of course huge variations either side of this). Guto was at his best in the early 1700s, which is a shame, as it would be nice to have him as the record holder on some of our races (and not even Penmaenmawr dates back that far). He was so fast that 'he could catch a bird in flight', and was said to have been easily capable of running from his home in Llwyncelyn to Pontypridd and back in the time it took his mother to boil the kettle, so Kenny Stuart's Snowdon record might well have been threatened by a Welshman.

Ras Cnicht – post-race relaxation in the slate swimming pool

The Preseli Hills are right out on the margins of the Welsh fell running tradition, far removed from the drama of Snowdonia or the runnable tracks of the Beacons. A degree of commitment is required for the average runner to make it out this far to the outer fringes of the Welsh upland landscape. They are small hills (although usually called 'mountains' by locals), with the highest point just a tad over 500 metres, but what they lack in height they make up for in variety of terrain and the intangible mystery of the landscape. The Bluestones of Stonehenge were famously sourced here, and the landscape is riddled with tumuli and burial chambers, like Carreg Coetan and the incomparable Pentre Ifan (described by Julian Cope as 'the most elegant, mesmerising and just plain large dolmen on the British mainland'). The ancient Golden Road traverses the spine of the hills; and what could be more alluring to a red-blooded mountain runner than that name?

But because of that geographical marginality, races down here in the south-west have traditionally been few and far between. Ras Beca, which we have already covered, was one highly unusual exception, but when Maenclochog local Carwyn Phillips started running in the nearby hills there was very little else.

'Pembrokeshire had a big road running scene, and to be honest that's how I started – I used to love it – but once I started running off-road in the Preselis I just thought "wow, this is amazing". They quickly became my training ground', says Phillips, who brims with enthusiasm for his region and his sport. 'I thought: I'm going away for all these races, and yet I hardly ever saw anybody running in the Preselis. There was Ras Beca and that was it. You know, the races across Wales seemed to be getting longer and tougher and I just thought: I want to bring people to the village of Maenclochog to run on the Preselis.'

The result was the **Preseli Beast**, a product of Carwyn's in-depth knowledge of the terrain, as well as his taste for the longer routes. It was launched in 2012, and became the longest race ever to feature in the Welsh fell running championships five years later. That May, a group of us Flintshire runners formed a raiding party and travelled down for it. We were enthused, to say the least. 'You could just tell that the route had been planned by somebody with intimate knowledge of the area', said Hayley Evans as we regrouped after the race. 'It's not just the hills, it's the variety'.

Carwyn explains his thought processes when trying to formulate a long race in the unlikely and previously 'untested' terrain of the south-west: 'Even when I was going away to race I was thinking, "well this is good but the Preselis are just as good". They're obviously not as big but they can still be tough and I just wanted to bring people down for something other than the beaches.' There was an evangelical side to it too, a desire to spread the love, to encourage locals on to their nearby hills. 'I just got really excited about that, but also about helping, or nurturing, people around here to think about running off-road. The people I spoke to said "oh I don't know, I'd get lost" so that's why I started The Beast as a marked route to give them the confidence to run off road so they could see what they could do, what's out there for them, and try to give them a variety of terrain rather than just fell.'

Long fell races like the Preseli Beast require a special kind of commitment: they are not events to be tackled lightly, which is why the organisers of them will generally insist on some evidence of previous experience. It is also why the kit requirements are often rigidly adhered to, and much stricter than those in shorter races. The 'Longs' are a class apart, and it often takes some time for people new to the sport to be able to make that step up, even if they have a background in marathons or other forms of serious distance running.

The essence of the challenge of the 'Longs' is three-fold, particularly when they are held in the higher mountains of the north-west. First, and most fundamentally, is the fact that multiple hills need to be climbed, not just one or two. This takes a certain amount of self-control, as it is even more critical to eke out reserves of energy on a long fell race than it is on a road marathon. Often, you hear of runners who really struggle to make the transition from a single hill dash – one relatively short sustained effort – to the demands of multiple peaks.

It also takes considerable endurance allied to the ability to eat, and (equally importantly) hold down, food. Second: the terrain, which might be awkward on shorter races but is at least short-lived. On long races, like Pedol Peris, that terrain becomes a key factor, with a lot of bare rock over Elidir Fawr, Glyder Fawr, Lliwedd and Snowdon, and very few comfortably runnable sections unless you are well-used to the high mountain environment. Third: the conditions, which are rarely ideal and which may well change during the race, such is the scale of the undertaking. Navigation and route-finding are the final ingredients to be added to that heady broth: all of which combine to make all the 'Longs' particularly satisfying tests of hill-craft combined with fitness.

Wales has fewer classic 'longs'

Elidir

than the Lakes. Sometimes – rather absurdly – this leads runners to the peculiar conclusion that the mountains are 'easier'. In fact, of course, it is the opposite: it is not really feasible to race over the tops of Tryfan, or Crib Goch, because the terrain is just that little bit too awkward (although there are exceptions, as we will see).

In the Lake District, the classic longs are well known, much sought after 'ticks' that any fell runner would wish to add to their CV, even if only to experience them once. The likes of Borrowdale, Wasdale, Duddon and Ennerdale are superb races: all are horseshoes, and all are hard grassroots fell races, grittily traditional and defiantly not-for-profit.

In Snowdonia, the two established 'longs' also have legendary status, but both are very different from the Lakes races, as well as from each other. Pedol Peris (the Pedol horseshoe), generally takes place in September

1. Welsh 3000s, descending from Glyder Fach;
2. Foel Goch from Ogwen

(so it will be covered later, as it just slips into autumnal status), with the **Welsh 1000 metre peaks** race normally run in early June.

The 1000s has an interesting history – quite unlike that of any other Welsh mountain race. It was established as a military training route after the Welsh Fusiliers were accused of contributing to erosion by their practise of using the Welsh 3000s route as a training ground, in full battle dress including heavy military boots. In 1971 it was run as a formal race for the first time, with 19 entrants, won by Dennis Weir in 3 hours 47 minutes. The greatest fell runner of all time, Lake District farmer Jos Naylor, took 10 minutes off that time the next year; and the race later came to be dominated by Colin Donnelly, a Scotsman who ran for Eryri Harriers for many years.

There is something particularly intimidating about the linear nature of the 1000s, especially for the kind of runner that finds their way to the hills from road running, rather than a background in mountaineering or climbing. A runner like Jez Brown of Buckley, in fact, who remembers waiting in the field in Abergwyngregyn, on the peaceful shores of the Menai Straits, at the start of his first Welsh 1000 metres race as if it was yesterday.

'I'm not an experienced mountain walker or climber, I just enjoy running. I like to run in nice places and to challenge myself,' says Brown. 'I'd done hundreds of races by this point, but this was one I was really nervous about.' Was this, I wonder, due to the seriousness and commitment of the course? Unlike most races, even most of the long ones, you can't just 'cut it short' and return back to your car, because your car is in Llanberis, along with everybody elses (a bus takes runners to the sea level start). Worse than that, even if you do decide to drop out, you have to reach the first road in Ogwen at the very least, and that is a long haul from Aber over the highest peaks of the Carneddau.

'Yes, but thinking about it, this was more than just nerves, or excitement about the nature of the route,' said Brown. 'So many things can go wrong in a long distance race over rough terrain, and I was really aware of that when we set off from the coast. I wasn't thinking about position or time, I know my limitations, I just wanted to get to the top of Snowdon without getting lost, without cramping up, or becoming exhausted, making sure I had enough to eat and to drink along the way, to manage the trickier rock scrambling sections, and to enjoy it.' Jez is a modest man; he is actually a talented athlete who dealt well with the course and rightly concluded that it 'is not so much a race, more an adventure over the best that Snowdonia has to offer, and one I have done a few times now, in the best and worst of conditions.'

The worst of conditions can be very bad indeed. The Gorphwysfa Club now organises it, and one can only imagine how difficult some of the decisions they have had to make regarding this race have been over the years.

The 2009 race was a case in point. I battled my way through the race that year in very tough conditions: howling wind, some unusually vicious gusts, a dank chill in the air, sleet at times, finishing in a raging storm on top of Yr Wyddfa. One of the many unique features of the race is that finish: on top of Snowdon itself, so there is little opportunity in these conditions to rest or recuperate. Instead, it is a question of putting on all spare kit and evacuating as soon as possible. So, I scampered back down the tourist path to my car in Llanberis; an extra six-mile 'warm-down' to add to the 22 mile race. The weather had been bad, and I guessed that a lot of people had retired, but I was completely oblivious to anything more than that, and certainly oblivious to any media interest. This, I think, was for two reasons: partly because these kinds of conditions are not all that unusual in the Welsh hills, but mainly because I ran the race on my own (in a one-man bubble of mist and rain, which is what happens in these circumstances, focused entirely on the moment, on navigation and on coping with the conditions) and travelled back on my own too.

It was only later that I experienced a weird sense of deja vu as I relaxed, blissfully warm and dry, with pint in hand, putting my feet up and switching on the BBC news. And there it was: journalists and eye-witnesses reporting from a 'mountain race in Snowdonia', tales emerging of abandonment and rescues, runners lost and injured, the usual disjuncture between truth and journalistic license playing out again.

The deja vu was because it had only been seven months since the 2008 OMM, which I had also competed in, and which was still fresh in my mind. That particular weekend entered into mountain running folklore – it was the first time that an event of that nature had jumped from the pages of the specialist press into mainstream consciousness, and certainly the first time a mountain race had taken over the news agenda.

Without going into too much detail (because it was in Borrowdale in the Lake District) the event, which is deliberately scheduled for the last weekend in October in an effort to increase its difficulty (coping with adverse conditions being a fundamental requirement) was hit by one of those biblical late autumn storms which affect the western hills of the British Isles particularly badly. This one was notably ferocious. My memories are fragmentary, but I can remember linking arms with my partner Paul McCullough and another pair (the OMM is an event for teams of two) in a futile effort to avoid getting blown over as we crossed the exposed summit of Dale Head. Howling gales and barely credible volumes of water characterised the first day – but we struggled through, got to all the checkpoints on the shortened course, pitched our tent at the overnight camp in Buttermere, got a brew on, and tried to ignore the constant buffeting of the ferocious wind. Minutes later, the call came through by loud-hailer: the event had been abandoned for the first time in its 50 year history. As we emerged from the tent, it instantly took off, ripped from its moorings in the gales, spiralling into the upper atmosphere and presumably ended up in the Urals. I never saw it again.

We were blown over multiple times (and occasionally dragged along the ground) as we battled back over Honister to our car in Borrowdale, only to find the entire valley flooded and cars floating downstream. The BBC covered it extensively for over 24 hours using the headline '2000 runners unaccounted for'. The millionaire owner of the Honister Pass tourist attractions, Mark Weir (who later died in a helicopter crash) sensed some free publicity. Understanding the importance of a media-friendly soundbite, he memorably claimed that 'the organisers were within an inch of turning the Lake District into a morgue'. In reality, you are never safer running in the hills than you are on a mountain marathon, for the obvious reason that you are required to carry a significant amount of kit: self-sufficiency in the hills is the entire point. One person sprained his ankle and the rest of us just had an uncomfortable night and another splendid anecdote to bore people rigid with.

It was, therefore, distinctly odd to have been involved in both (indeed, my presence at races was deemed something of 'a warning' for at least a year). Doggedly completing the Welsh 1000s that year remains my only ever top 10 finish at the event, so as far as I'm concerned it was entirely legitimate. Over 50 in the fell runners class retired (many forced to stop at Ogwen), with similar proportions retiring in the other six classes. The event retains its military link – with special categories for the army, and for 'mountaineers' (who are still forced to wear boots of a certain weight).

To pile coincidence on coincidence, 2009 was also the year in which the **Foel Fras** race – which takes a sweeping loop around the hills of the northern Carneddau – was hit by a dramatic squall at the worst possible moment, just as most of the runners were at the highest, most remote part of the course approaching the obscure knoll of Yr Aryg. For Jez Brown, this was another formative experience still seared into his memory after hundreds of subsequent races: 'This race, at the height of summer, started with mild conditions near the sea in Abergwyngregyn. After the gradual five mile climb up to the top of Drum and Foel Fras driving hailstorms with terrible visibility led to a significant number of runners including me being unable to find the checkpoint on the top of the summit,' says Brown.

I was at the race too, and have vivid memories of shivering runners struggling to squeeze into tiny pairs

1. Foel Fras; 2. Cwm Dulyn bothy, a good base for Carneddau runs

of waterproof trousers at the height of the mini-storm on top of Foel Fras. Brown had an even more dramatic experience: 'I was with another runner who was struggling to put his waterproofs on due to the freezing and windy conditions, and needed urgent help to get off the mountain. I tried to help him but I suddenly cramped up, falling to the floor and struggling to get up again – not the best place to be in those conditions.'

The camaraderie of the sport comes to the fore at times like this. I have seen, and heard, of many incidents where runners have sacrificed their own race to help injured rivals. It happens fairly often: the sprained ankle, the deep cut, the hypothermia. We are all competitive, but we also look out for each other, a fundamental code of the mountain environment. For Brown, it was 'the first and only time I have ever used the whistle that I must have carried for thousands of miles, and thankfully this was replied to with other whistles from the marshals who were actually not too far from us. Race positions, times, and completing the route were totally forgotten about as a group of us then got off the summit as quickly as we could and got back to the warmth of the race HQ and the welcome soup and roll.' There isn't much that can't be cured with hot soup, and Yr Hen Felin – a converted mill in Abergwyngregyn – is a convivial spot in which to gradually thaw out and begin to swap stories.

On Bera Mawr in the northern Carneddau

There are, for me, two ways in which a mountain race becomes a classic. Both are to do with the purity of the line – and in this sense there are further parallels with rock climbing. As we have already established, it is no coincidence that many fell runners are also climbers, or found their way to one sport from the other. There is something about the nature of what a climber would call a 'natural line' and a fell runner would call a 'great route' that relates to its aesthetic quality – there is a beauty and a purity to a classic rock climb that is often obvious even to non-climbers. Similarly, an obvious horseshoe like that which encircles the Llanberis Pass has a compelling quality, a beauty and a purity that presents an irresistible challenge to a certain kind of person.

The Lakes have more 'horseshoe' races than we do in Wales, partly because of geography and topography.

But we have a few classics: and **Pedol Peris** (the **Peris Horseshoe**) is at the top of the list for most runners, an essential addition to the CV that often takes several years to build up to.

Races like Moel Siabod and Snowdon are obvious classics in terms of the nature of their 'challenge', in the sense that you start at the bottom, get to the top of the peak and run back as quickly as possible. Horseshoes are not quite that obvious, but for those with an eye for landscape the shadow of the Nant Peris skyline haunts the drive towards Llanberis. It is always there on the horizon, winking at you from the road through Deiniolen and Penisarwaun. It is undoubtedly the classic Welsh long, and one of the greatest mountain races in the British Isles. Regulars just know it as *the* Pedol, with no further explanation necessary – it is the horseshoe, the definitive essence of the form.

Nant Peris

I used to keep a photograph of myself approaching the summit of Yr Wyddfa at the business end of the Pedol as a reminder of how bad things can get if you miscalculate a long fell race. My face was a shade of double-

Descending from Y Garn to Nant Peris in heavy rain

cream with mauve blotches; I look dreadfully ill. It was the first time I'd done the full race, in 2008 perhaps, with my friend and then training partner Neil Parry. We both made a classic error, underestimating the final section over Lliwedd and failing to take on enough water at the Pen y Pass road crossing (the half-way point).

A nightmare ensued, familiar to all distance runners. Dehydration worsens, eating then becomes impossible, and a downward spiral kicks in as energy reserves become dangerously depleted. Cyclists, and some runners, know this glycogen depletion as the 'bonk', but that doesn't really convey quite how bad it can get in the mountains, where the nature of the terrain presents additional problems, and the symptoms of depletion can be much more general. I still remember Kean and Sandra Rowlands offering me a drink below the final scramble up the edge of Clogwyn y Garnedd – the quickest way for runners to get to the top of Snowdon from Bwlch y Saethau. It was no accident that the couple, fell running legends both, chose to stand there – they knew we would be suffering at that precise point. Those few ambrosial mouthfuls remain ingrained in my memory (although at the time they were absorbed by my desperate physiology all too quickly).

At the top of the rocky climb that takes a direct route up Yr Wyddfa, that photograph was taken – becoming, for me, the epitome of what it means to struggle. Since then, I've heard numerous stories and seen numerous incidents on the same race – from phenomenal performances like Gavin Bland's 3.04 in 1994, and Menna Angharad's 3.28 in 1996 (said by those in the know to be one of the most impressive fell running feats of all time), through to more basic tactics involving a five pound note, a cake and a pint of hot chocolate at the Pen y Pass café.

Big Richie Evans, a regular at the Colomendy pub, the spiritual home of north-east Wales fell running, does not have the typical fell runners build. But he is as tough as they come, and decided he wanted to run the Pedol. It was a bad weather year, low cloud, wind, rain: all the usual ingredients.

But Richie took it in his stride as he is impervious to cold, just a vest will suffice in all but the direst weather. It was going well until Lliwedd, after which his energy levels crashed, so he decided to abandon the race and take the quickest route back to Llanberis. Cresting the top of the zigzags by the infamous obelisk, the weather worsened, as it often does, exposed to the full force of the westerlies. Exhausted, and disorientated, he headed down as quickly as possible, only realising he was actually heading to Beddgelert, in the opposite direction, when it was too late. Just above the village, he met a couple of walkers who offered to drive him round to Llanberis (a considerable distance, as any Snowdonian tourist quickly discovers). He was in a bad way, and tells a story about what happened next: as his seatbelt was unclipped by his new friends on arrival in Llanberis, he dropped out of the car like a bag of sand, lying in the foetal position on the grass verge outside the

Victoria Hotel, barely audible groans suggesting to concerned onlookers that he'd probably live to fight another day.

Legendary Llanberis club Eryri Harriers have always been associated with the Pedol, and it retains its core principles: it is the very essence of a long, hard mountain race which embodies all the key principles of the sport. Founded in 1977 by Snowdon race organiser Ken Jones and a small team of enthusiasts, Eryri essentially pioneered mountain running in north Wales, inculcating a genuine grassroots culture from the outset. That spirit is maintained by stalwart race organisers like Mike Blake, Arwel Lewis, Ellie Salisbury and many others.

For a few glorious years, it was accompanied (earlier in summer) by **Ras Pedol Cwm Pennant**, another long horseshoe around that most beautiful of valleys hidden away in the south-western corner of the national park. So beautiful, in fact, that Eifion Wyn celebrated it in a famous englyn:

the final lines of which will resonate with any mountain runner:

> Pam, Arglwydd, y gwnaethost Gwm Pennant mor dlws?
> A bywyd hen fugail mor fyr?

> Why, Lord, did you make Cwm Pennant so beautiful?
> And the life of an old shepherd so short?

In its brief span of a few years, the life of the race was even shorter than that of an old shepherd. It assumed legendary status, however, noted in particular for the arduous nature of its final descent down tussocky Cwm Ciprwth from Garnedd Goch at the end of the Nantlle ridge. It even featured as a British Championship race in 2016, with the cream of British fell running talent lured by its reputation, and its links with one of the elite Gwynedd runners good enough to mix it with the best of them, Matthew Roberts.

Apart from Pedol and the 1000s, the other Welsh 'longs' are all in the south, where the kinder terrain and rolling ridges lend themselves to classic loops. The previously mentioned Llanbedr-Blaenafon just nudges into the category, while the Preseli Beast massively exceeds it, being almost marathon distance. The Black Mountains and the Brecon Beacons also each boast one summer 'long'. Both are esoteric, both are hard, both attract small fields of tough devotees.

The closest I have ever been to shedding real tears when running was the **Black Mountains** race in the September of 2014. I'd been chasing the Welsh championships again that year, the season was drawing to a close, and was having a good race by my less-than-stellar standards. The race is wonderfully runnable over the limestone summits of Pen Cerrig Calch and Pen Allt Mawr – from which bare top you can see over to the final ridge of **Waun Fach** (sometimes called the 'Dragon's Back', taken by the unheralded but brilliant short race of the same name every summer – so low key that it doesn't even have any prizes5). I reached the final summit of Crug Mawr in 2.35, to be told by the optimistic marshal that it was '10 minutes to the finish'. This was my chance – stomach cramps couldn't spoil the final descent, pelting down to the finish and glory. Then came a crossroads. No tape. No other runners. No obvious onward route. Panic.

I waited several minutes for the next runner, and followed him straight down to some tape marking the final descent. This was a relief, so I switched off again – a big mistake – and concentrated on sprinting to the finish, inadvertently flying past the final stile as the red mist descended, ploughing down the minor road towards Crickhowell when I should have been finishing with a decent time. I had to navigate my way back along the river, haemorrhaging time and deeply frustrated (I'd been leading the V40 category of the championships until that moment).

I was later told the descent from Crug Mawr is the exact reverse of the climb on Llanbedr-Blaenafon, so perhaps I have few excuses. At the time, however, it was a pretty demoralising error so close to the finish, and it was impossible for me to close the gap with leader Darren Fishwick on the last race, the time-honoured season-closer up **Rhobell Fawr** from the tiny village of

Llanfachreth above Dolgellau. This latter event is the ultimate autumn race, because Llanfachreth is perhaps the best place in Wales to enjoy the sight of leaves on the turn, graced as it is with acres of sessile oak woodland, a glimpse into the natural heritage of Wales, a reminder of what our country should look like.

But before we head back north, another race and a miniature final anecdote from the Black Mountains speaks to the human dimensions of the sport, far removed from the impersonal razzle dazzle of a big city marathon. 'The close-knit nature of the sport, and the community that we're all part of really hit me on this race,' says Peter Agnew, a long-term fell and ultra runner from Mold who also ran it that same year. 'I was ploughing along, speeding up a little as we began the homeward leg, when my mind started drifting and I

Brecon Beacons fell race 2019
(pic: Jane Aggleton)

noticed a set of footprints that I recognised. That's Andrea Rowlands (a leading female runner, multiple winner of the Welsh Championships), I thought, and soon enough she came into view. It seemed to say something about the dimensions of the sport, that in a field of 100, and with enough time on your hands, you even start to recognise people's footprints.'

The other big horseshoe in the south is the **Brecon Beacons fell race**. It's a bit of a stretch describing this as autumnal, as it usually takes place in late August, but it can get pretty nippy at night that time of year – and the dank hollow of the campsite near the Youth Hostel chilled us to the bone when we stayed there before the race in 2019. It certainly felt like autumn as I dashed from tent to toilet in the early hours. As is often the case at that time of year, the cold, clear night heralded a perfect late summer day. Perfect for hillwalkers that is. For us, it was immediately obvious that the day would be a struggle against dehydration. There's virtually no running water on the Beacons ridge, and the classic route takes a giant loop around the reservoirs that form a chain up the valley from Talybont-on-Usk. Each year, organiser Gary Davies alternates directions, but whichever way you go the start is steep to gain the main Beacons ridge. In 2019, it headed up to Carn Pica first, a long, long haul before an even longer haul over the main peaks (which, on this glorious day, had so many walkers on them that it was hard to find the race marshals) to the first water at Upper Neuadd. It is almost impossible in these circumstances to take on enough water – and the weight penalty of carrying too much outweighs the benefits of hydration for most mountain runners. The return leg is a daunting prospect in this heat, close to 10 miles over awkward twisting hills back towards the end of the reservoir above

Brecon Beacons

Two Hillforts

Talybont. A few casualties of the heat were wilting on the hidden tracks below Bryniau Gleision, and by the time we reached the last checkpoint on the summit of Tor y Foel we were reduced to basic survival mode, sharing out tiny portions of water proffered by the saintly marshal. Stuart Thomas, who broke his back in a car crash in his youth, chose this day to do his first proper long fell race – painkillers and dehydration combining to make it a character-building experience, although he finished in good time without the slightest complaint. It's worth noting how the basic, self-sufficient ethos of the sport is embraced and valued even by those who are relatively new to it.

This time of year, on the cusp of late summer and early autumn sees the racing calendar packed, with organisers intent on squeezing out the last of the daylight and kind conditions before the rigours of winter. The Clwydian Hills host some lovely little races at this time, like Joe Cooper's **Two Hillforts** which embraces the Iron Age heritage that is so obvious around the summits of Moel Arthur and Pen y Cloddiau. And Tim Hargreaves' **King John's Castle**, conceived by local runner John Linley as an homage to local history in its painfully steep journey from the secluded village of Llanarmon yn Ial. It even finishes on the ancient motte of Tomen y Faerdre – built by the lords of Ial (anglicised as Yale – the family benefactors lending their name to the famous university in New

England), then rebuilt by English King John in the thirteenth century as he took on the mighty Welshman Llywellyn ap Iorwerth ('Llywellyn the Great').

If the Clwydian hills are too gentle, head west. In the heartland above Llanberis lurks the brutal **Elidir Fawr**, almost certainly the hardest single climb of any Welsh race, packing 2800ft of ascent into its 8km length. It is now held at a standard time on a Saturday afternoon, but in 2016 Dyfed Whiteside Thomas experimented by holding it in the evening of the 1st of September just as the long summer evenings give way to the gloom of autumn. It gave a truly memorable outing in fading light, battling up that dreadful climb into the mist, plotting a way through the boulder-strewn summit before enjoying the wonderful looping descent around Cwm Brwynog. This is always very fast, and on that evening it was into a headwind, with mist swirling around Crib Goch across the Pass. 'Rage against the dying of the light' seemed an appropriate, if not entirely original, mantra for the final steep drop down the spur to some well-earned bara brith, and a pint in the Vaynol.

5 Quite unexpectedly, the descent down Y Grib (the 'Dragon's Back') on the Waun Fach race turned into one of the best mountain running experiences I've ever had in almost 600 races: all this from a tiny event in the Black Mountains with entries taken for £3 in a barn (preferable to the increasingly commercialised Snowdon race that was, at the time, held on the same day). I thought I'd been everywhere in the Welsh mountains, north and south, but I'd never been on this final ridge: the descent was superb, the racing exciting, and the race seemed to me to be the very definition of 'grassroots'.

Road running has a tendency to attract people who are busy reinventing themselves: those who formerly had a drinking problem, the overweight, the mentally unstable. I say this with my tongue partly in my cheek (I have done hundreds of road races, and have loved it ever since doing my first half marathon just before my 13th birthday in 1983: this would now be seen as child cruelty). But there is definitely an element of truth to the assertion, and it is exploited by advertisers who see such people, and the egos they bring along, as naturally attracted to the kind of meaningless inspirational slogans that clog up advertising and social media. There are those for whom nothing has really happened unless it can be accompanied by a gurning selfie complete with air-headed slogan: all of which has been co-opted, packaged, and mobilised by commerce: 'be all you can be', 'find your epic', 'impossible is nothing', 'livestrong'. Leave all grammatical rules behind and hope to attract some attention.

I wonder how many of those types are here tonight? We are in the hills above the highest village in Wales on a dark and snowy night in December: there is no obvious reason why any normal person would be up here. I have been doing these night-time races, the '**Dashes in the Dark**', through the woods and hills above Llandegla, for over 12 years. They have always been organised by various incarnations of the admirable Clwydian Range Runners club, and I can remember fields as small as 25 in the past: indeed there was a time when I regularly finished 2nd at these races, which must say something.

Dash in the Dark, Llandegla (pic: Steve Jeffery)

Tonight, however, there are 193 runners, and many of those are certainly not standard-issue fell runners. On one level, this is wonderful, of course it is. On another, I fret about the consequences. Fell running, as a sport, has not traditionally sought to attract participants. The British mountains are small in scale, there is really not much upland space to go around – and so the reasons for keeping things low key are obvious. A couple of years ago I ran the Burbage Skyline fell race on a summer evening in the Peak District (but very close to the urban fringe of Sheffield). Over 450 turned up, for a race that takes a series of narrow paths as it negotiates a series of gritstone edges; far too many for the nature of the terrain, it meant that it was impossible to break into an actual run until we were half way round the course.

So I wonder why we are all here tonight: is it just people 'finding their epic' by running round some snowy woods in the dark with a torch? Are they doing this for the love of it, or just to boast and post?

Not for the first time, before or since, my cynicism was misplaced[6]. Nobody was there for the wrong reasons, all were there to enjoy themselves and pit themselves against the elements on a cold winter's night. It's better than staring at a screen, after all. There's a party atmosphere before, during and after the race: the rewards for getting out on a foul night in the middle of winter are obvious, and I chide myself for being utterly wrong, yet again. As usual after this event, we retire to the Rose and Crown in the tiny village of Griaianrhyd, a superb pub that is second only to the mighty Colomendy in the affections of north-east Wales fell runners. It serves legendary chip butties, the size of pillows, alongside some perfectly kept real ale.

[6] In 2016, I was phoned by Clair Atterbury, a new runner from Prestatyn, who wondered whether my Hotfoot up Famau race might be suitable as a first fell race. It is hard to give a fair answer in these circumstances, and I hate to patronise anybody, so she ended up running. She struggled, recording the slowest ever time: the midsummer sun set over Snowdonia as she climbed the gully, surrounded by an entourage of marshalls. I wasn't sure whether she would ever race in the hills again. A year later, two friends of mine, Tim Hargreaves and Paul Aird, both alerted me to the fact that not only had Clair come back, but she was winning races, and the lean athlete now featuring in dozens of race photographs was genuinely unrecognisable. Clair is now a top female runner.

Earlier in November comes the first race that feels like a 'winter' event: the **Penmaenmawr fell race**. It is arguably the oldest proper mountain race in Wales, many people regard it as such, and it has always been something of a coda to the main season. It is also somewhat atypical as a mountain race in the sense that it doesn't take in any summits, but instead involves an extended loop around Tal y Fan – a self-effacing and eminently runnable peak that is very noticeable from Conwy. Other races go to the summit of this lovely little hill – the **Gladstone 9** (in September) from the eponymous pub in Dwygyfylchi, and the **Tal y Fan** race (in July) connected to the Rowen show – but the 'Pen race' is by far the best known.

One year, 2006 perhaps, the wind was so fierce that little Pete Roberts, a Buckley clubmate of mine weighing no more than nine stone in his stockinged feet, was blown off his feet, landing in a patch of old snow, dusting himself off and continuing as if nothing could be more natural. On other years we've often plunged through the deep bog that makes the far side of the course hard going in 'wet years' (most of them), or glide along the top of the bog, with the ground frozen like concrete (considerably rarer). The donkey track finish is steep, narrow and hazardous, luring those at the sharp end into taking the odd risk. 'One of my proudest wins came a few years back at this race – it was just a wonderful run,' says Jez Brown, after I asked him to reminisce about one of his favourite races. 'I was in a group of three out in front, chatting with the other two, who I knew quite well, none of us seeming to want to break away, working well as a group and staying out in front. After nine miles of this, at the top of the donkey track, I thought "well, I might as well give it a go", as nobody else seemed keen to make their move. So I threw caution to the wind, heading out into the

1. *Lightweight 'runners bivouac' on Cadair Berwyn; 2. Descending to Cwm Maen Gwynedd at the height of 'Storm Barbara'*

bracken, a wild dash to the finish, and then jumping back on to the narrow slippery path in front of them.'

There is something very special about this part of the northern Carneddau. Julian Cope's books on megalithic Britain outline its archaeological importance: there was clearly something about this landscape that spoke to our ancestors – the land is saturated with meaning, the place names redolent of a past so ancient that it fires the imagination. It is a wonderful environment in which to run. Stone circles, ancient tracks, and burial chambers abound – Bwlch y Ddeufaen, for example, the two huge obelisks warm to the touch, standing at the lip of the obvious pass between Rowen and Abergwyngregyn. Less obvious, but just as precious, is the Neolithic burial chamber of Maen y Bardd, the poet's stone, a remote dolmen with its bulky capstone resting on four standing stones. Less obvious still are the multiple smaller sites scattered around the slopes of Tal y Fan and Pen y Castell, like Cerrig Pryfaid, Waun Bryn Gwenith and Maen Penddu. Prehistoric tracks, older than recorded history, link all these ancient places, and weave across this spectacular landscape in bewildering complexity. For Jez Brown, it is 'a place made for running'.

The Pen race celebrated its 40th anniversary in 2014. Brown knew this: 'the long history meant that to add my name to the list of winners was very special. The race attracts runners from all over the place – it's not just for fell runners, you see road runners and triathletes who want to give this fell running business a try.'

As the days shorten, and the weather worsens, the races tail off. That doesn't mean we stop running, of course: some of the most memorable days in the hills are those of midwinter, often in the company of a small group of like-minded friends, people unlikely to complain about a spot of 'weather'. The Berwyn ridge at the height of Storm Barbara, the old Carneddau race route in thick snow, a loop of Foel Fras in constant sleet on the shortest day of the year, with Aber Falls a wall of white water: the memories stay with you. And a few idiosyncratic races continue – there are several in the border hills of Shropshire, most notably the competitive Cardington Cracker which draws hundreds of athletes from a very wide radius. There is also the unique **Jubilee Plunge**, which starts at the eponymous tower on top of Moel Famau and – as its name suggests – descends at full pelt to the Golden Lion pub in Llangynhafal on the Vale of Clwyd side. I am not the only person that takes longer to recover from this two mile downhill dash than I do to recover from a road marathon: at least a week of aching quadriceps and calves, as it is impossible not to be tempted to overstride as the racing red mist descends. It isn't the only 'downhill' race either – the legendary **Tryfan Downhill** takes place in August, organised by the record holder Mike Blake, famous for his eight minute descent from Adam and Eve to Ogwen in 1990 during which he broke at least one wrist.

1. *Aber Falls in a storm;*
2. *Carneddau race route*

Overleaf: Llyn Eigiau in the Carneddau, a landscape made for running

In short, this sport is multi-faceted. There are any number of specialisms to pursue, any number of directions that may favour one set of physical attributes or another. My own inclination has always been to embrace the lot, and if that means being average at everything, then so be it. The talented will always be able to match their attributes to a specialism and excel at that: some have a yen for the short and brutal, some for the long and arduous. For the latter group, there are multiple challenges in the Welsh hills that do not require the traditionalist to embrace the dark world of the commercially driven event (these are increasingly common: there are some ultra-marathons across the Welsh mountains that charge an entry fee in excess of £100 – needless to say, there is no place for them in this book).

The Welsh 3000s, the longest-established and most famous example of an obvious mountain running 'challenge', is free. Even short-distance specialists give it a go at least once, because it is a classic line with its basic 'rules' established back in 1919, when it was first completed in a single day by Eustace Thomas, 'the greyhound of the groughs'. His time of 22 hours wasn't that impressive, even in the heavy boot context of the era, and was slashed to eight hours, 25 minutes by Thomas Firbank and friends in 1938. Firbank wrote about his feat in his book 'I Bought a Mountain', although his predictions for future times proved amusingly wide of the mark: 'Somebody special, some great day, might break seven and a half...let us say that his time might be seven hours, twenty nine minutes, fifity nine seconds.'[7] By the early 1970s, Jos Naylor did it in less than five, and this was reduced to 4.19 by émigré Scotsman Colin Donnelly supported by a crack team of Eryri Harriers in 1988. This stood for over 30 years before another Scot, Finlay Wild, took an enormous eight minutes off it in May 2019.

Llyn Edno on the Paddy Buckley route

By coincidence, I had just got back from traversing the Cuillin ridge on Skye when I heard about Wild's feat. My time across the ridge was less than impressive, and my mind was already boggling with Wild's much-publicised record Cuillin time (a barely credible 2.59.22 for those taking notes) as I took the long road home. Indeed, in another coincidence it was also on my mind because his name came up as I chatted to a chap on the tiny second belay ledge of the classic rock climb Ardverikie Wall, which we did on our way up to Skye. Finlay Wilde was his GP, he said, an ego-shattering experience for any mountain enthusiast, boggling at a life that manages to combine career and passion so successfully (he certainly maximises his leave – while he was in north Wales, Wild also took three minutes off Gareth Wyn Hughes' Snowdon Horseshoe record of 1.23.48.)

Beyond the 3000s, the possibilities for ultra-long days in the Welsh mountains are limitless, and beyond the scope of this book. The Dragon's Back stage race across the length of upland Wales is well known, and even generates a certain amount of wider publicity, as does the iconic Paddy Buckley Round[8], which is growing in popularity and reputation year-on-year. Somewhat more obscure (and, some say, tougher) is the Meirionydd Round, while an easier option for those less committed to these monumental undertakings is the 'Sea-to-Sea', which heads from Porthmadog to Conwy over the 25 peaks of the Moelwynion and Carneddau.

At the end of that particular outing, Peter Agnew and I ran past the Albion and down to the Conwy waterfront, descending the jetty in front of the Liverpool Arms to stand in the sea, in beautiful evening sunshine, just under 13 hours after dipping our feet in Cardigan Bay this morning. It all worked perfectly: the route was as satisfying, elegant and meaningful as I had hoped it would be.

It hadn't all been plain sailing. An inevitable feature of very long runs is the good patch, bad patch cycle, which rarely coincides when you are in a team of two. 'Good job you're here', I heard Peter say to Hayley Evans (who had supported us from Capel) as we got to the trig point on Foel Fras. 'Otherwise I would have killed him'. On other occasions, however, he surged ahead, with me struggling to stay in touch – it's always the way, spirits and energy levels ebb and flow, there are good times and there are bad times, but the pain eventually passes. They are a rather obvious metaphor for life itself and, as such, arguably an essential part of any well-lived life. On that day, the final trig point on Tal y Fan was decorated with a sheep's skull, which seemed appropriate.

Some runners just keep on going, and have a genetic affinity for the longer stuff. Again, details are beyond the scope of this book as hundreds of athletes have put in multiple incredible performances over many years. Some of these are well known and justifiably celebrated within the sport, others are low key, preferring to share the experience with just a few companions.

Two short anecdotes will have to suffice to explain the appeal. Carwyn Phillips dates his interest in multi-peak rounds back to an early encounter with a friend who ran cross-country with him. 'He said "oh you should start running up in the mountains". I didn't have a clue about map reading or anything like that so I went with him a couple of times and I just loved it. Mind blowing. So we did a couple of longish days out and I soon found out I was pretty good at the long stuff, so he said "oh you should think about the 3000s and the Paddy". These were unknown words for me at the time but it opened my mind. Then I supported someone on the Meirionydd Round, that was my first taste at supporting and I thought "this is just unbelievable", you're out in the hills all day, you get to eat loads of food, you're not racing against anybody like road running, and I just loved it. The supporting thing – just fantastic.'

Rounds like the Paddy and Meirionydd are of such a magnitude that it is standard to be supported for the entire route (although some do them solo). The basic principle was established by the Lake District's more famous Bob Graham round – the runner carries nothing, or the bare minimum, and the route is split into five different legs, all long and hard. The support team navigate, feed and generally take care of the aspirant. I had the honour of supporting Hayley Evans and Richard Bolton, who boldly undertook the Paddy in September 2019, right at the end of the feasible 'season' (although there have been a few winter rounds for the truly hardcore). The Moelwyn leg is a major outing in its own right, but after a bowl of soup in Nantmor, they both just kept on going, finishing some time in the next afternoon after a less-than-ideal night of wind and clag. For Hayley, who did the Bob Graham earlier that same year, it is all about the experience of spending time in the mountains with like-minded people, the sense of camaraderie that *really* long days engender is unique.

[7] Firbank was a Canadian by birth, but ended his days in Llanrwst's Dolanog nursing home. My Taid (from Penmachno) did too, and one day happened to mention that Firbank lived in the same corridor when he saw the book on a shelf at our house. It seemed unlikely that a Canadian would end up in this Welsh-speaking environment, but Firbank's mother came from the Berwyn Mountains, and he was apparently entirely at ease in Dolanog.

[8] The Paddy Buckley Round encompasses 47 summits on its 100km loop of Snowdonia, some 28,000ft of climbing – Everest from sea level, essentially, but with arduous descents added to the mix, and awkward terrain throughout. It is generally considered a tad harder than its better known Lake District equivalent, the Bob Graham Round. The

Meirionydd Round, devised and first completed by Yiannis Tridimas, is 72 miles long, with a little less climbing, but over even tougher terrain in the south of the National Park.

Descent from Carnedd Llywelyn

Postscript

Early morning in late October, and there's a blanket of cloud in Ogwen. Not a breath of wind, not too cold, a hint of humidity in the air. We park below the Milestone Buttress, and take our shoes out of the boot. This time of year, they are constantly wet from the incessant rain and unavoidable bog trotting, caked in mud and filth to the point that your feet are wet from the first stride. We lace up, and trot towards Capel Curig, turning off on the little path that cuts south towards Tryfan Bach, *little Tryfan*, that slabby nursery with the distinctive profile that has taught generations of novice climbers to make sure they avoid polished rock in the future.

Above, the ground gets wet, with cloying mud, then a blend of heather and boulders underfoot, making life awkward. We're already in the clag, which closes in around us as we climb, a silent descent, muffling all sound. It's a relatively gentle climb though, and it doesn't matter too much that we can't see anything: it's not as if we haven't been here before.

Cwm Brwynog then rears into a fairly steep headwall. On a good day, the East Face of Bristly Ridge is visible off to the right, with its unheralded and character-building rock climbs. To the left, the steep, forbidding black crag of Drws Nodded (its name is mysterious – something like 'door of refuge' – which I've always felt might refer to the possibility of sheltering under its giant overhang, taken by a horrific looking climb which bears an English name that's almost as good and almost as apposite as the Welsh name for the crag: Cobalt Dream).

We're moving more slowly now, much more slowly, as the angle steepens and the ground gets rough underfoot. I remember pelting down this path on the Rab Mountain Marathon of 2015; it was towards the end of the second day, I knew I was in with a chance of the Veteran prize and the red mist had descended. I'd picked up points at a checkpoint on the shores of Llyn Bochlwyd and was now intent on gaining the boggy ridge of the lower Glyderau, confident in 'local knowledge' to give me a bit of an advantage, heading for the impossible obscurity of re-entrants and other topographical ephemera hidden away above the untracked Dyffryn Mymbyr side of the ridge. This is the essence of the mountain marathon experience – no matter how much local knowledge you might think you have, the course planners find some ludicrously obscure locations for their checkpoints.

Today, however, there is no metaphorical red mist, just real mist. There's no need to race, or find any checkpoints. We are much calmer, the pace is gentle: it's far more pleasant.

At the top of the headwall, the thick clag begins to lighten, there's a distinct yellowish glow to it now, and we begin to see our shadows as we plod upwards. Things are looking promising: this is what we'd gambled on, this is what sometimes happens in these conditions at this time of year.

Then the magic begins. We pop through the mist, just below the top of the headwall below Bwlch Caseg Ffraith. Stretched out in front of us, a blanket of white cloud, all the valleys hidden but the tops clear. In fact, they are not just clear but uncannily radiant, crystalline, with every sculpted rock feature on the east face of Tryfan, so familiar, etched in perfect clarity. Every crack, every fissure, every ledge familiar from scores of rock climbs, scrambles and runs, over many decades.

It is a classic autumnal cloud inversion, and the rest of the day takes on a dreamlike quality, as we run suspended in space.

Above, across the Glyder plateau, the air is crisp, there's dew on the ground, and sunlight glistening off the distant Menai Strait. To the east, views over the cloud blanket to Moel Famau and the Clwydian hills of home. To the west, the cloud dissipates at the Irish Sea coast and beyond that we can make out a low dark line of crinkled peaks: the Wicklow Hills of Ireland.

Higher still, Glyder Fach. Its summit, a famously chaotic jumble of granite, is hidden by the upper reaches of the steep slope above us. I camped here once, on the shores of Llyn Caseg Fraith, another of my summer solstice solo trips. The next morning, very early, I trotted to the top of the nearby mountain, known as Foel Goch, or the Nameless Peak, and watched the sun rise at 4.45am (precisely: I checked my watch) above Llyn Cowlyd, which formed a perfect gap between Pen Llithrig y Wrach and Criegiau Gleision. It cast an orange glow, the sky multiple gradations of violet, lilac and purple.

The fact that we rush through a landscape doesn't mean that we don't appreciate it. I have never met a mountain runner who was not intimately attuned to the Welsh upland environment, its characteristics and its foibles. It is that knowledge, that intangible quality of 'experience' that is a central feature of fell running; and one of the reasons that the sport does not actively promote itself, does not 'reach out' in modern parlance, to new runners. It takes time to appreciate the varied demands and rewards of the sport, whether coming from road running or mountaineering, and the arena in which we run is inherently fragile.

*1., 2. & 3. Postscript Ogwen cloud inversion;
4. Climbing Pen Llithrig y Wrach*

That fragility extends to the communities that host the races. Rural villages across the remoter parts of Wales have their share of problems, and those are well documented: depopulation, linguistic sensitivity, poverty, lack of jobs. Outdoor sport cannot solve those problems, indeed it sometimes contributes to them, but running in the hills is more inclusive, more democratic, and far more accessible than the equipment-heavy technical sports that are sometimes credited with breathing economic life into rural Wales like rock-climbing, mountain biking or kayaking.

The races hidden away in the remote south-west, centred around the tight-knit village of Maenclochog in the Pembrokeshire interior, are good examples. As an event, the relatively new Preseli Beast has 'grown and grown', according to organiser Carwyn Phillips, who is rooted in the community. 'The villagers have really taken it to heart,' he adds. 'They love it. People say the support is great. It's really become a big thing in Maenclochog, people help out in different ways. They're always preparing for next year and they're so inspired that some of them have started running themselves: they were saying, "oh, these people are making all this effort to come down for our race – the least we can do is help out, cheer people on, or maybe even do it ourselves"'.

In my home area, the north-eastern fringe of Wales, our informal group of mountain runners has met every Friday evening for many years at the Colomendy in Cadole. It might well be the world's best pub, but it is self-effacing, hidden from the main Mold-Ruthin road down a narrow lane. Within its red brick walls we plan routes, trips and races, reminisce about past adventures and refuel with the best-kept cask ales in north Wales. Traditional non-dining pubs like this struggle to make ends meet, faced with multiple threats to their existence, from Wetherspoons to home drinking.

The demise of the British pub has been well documented. At the turn of the twentieth century, there were 100,000 pubs in Britain. Now, there are fewer than half that number, with 27 closing every week. The pub is also a rare example of genuine bottom-up folk culture in the UK, of something that is both nationally distinctive *and* egalitarian, inclusive (not always, but most of the time) and worthy of celebration. The Denbigh pubs of my youth were absolutely pure expressions of place, utterly authentic in the sense that nothing about them was staged, nothing was fake apart from the ersatz beams.

They are, in short, essential parts of community life, and it is no accident that the sport of fell running and the traditional British pub are inextricably intertwined. Both are grounded in place, both pride themselves on their lack of artifice and fuss. Many races start and finish at a particular pub, and the cultural links between the two has even been celebrated by breweries: neither the pub, nor the sport, have any truck with glossy commerciality or pretension. Cockermouth's Jennings, for example, and Northern Monk of Leeds, boast beers that explicitly riff on that link.

Two or three years ago, we decided to do something about the battle for survival those pubs are involved in (albeit in a small way, and only in the context of Flintshire). We decided to spread the love, adding a rotating Wednesday night 'away day' to Friday's Colomendy 'home fixture'. So, each Wednesday, a group of Buckley Runners (the local club I have been a member of since 2005) decide on a pub, which must meet minimum requirements in terms of beer quality, and have put together a sizeable portfolio of five to six mile routes that can be done all year round, with head-torches if necessary. At least 14 pubs across Flintshire now regularly find themselves hosting a filthy group of mountain runners on a regular basis: we see it as a form of charity.

Our regular routine from the Colomendy – the classic route – takes a path behind the pub to drop down to the leat (known to thousands of daytrippers to the Loggerheads park, which has lured Liverpudlians to its sylvan glades and babbling streams for well over a century). From here, we run up Moel Famau, maximising the effort needed to climb our local landmark. Come rain or shine, light or darkness, the routine continues, week in, week out: thousands of ascents over multiple decades. There are times, in the depths of winter, when the darkness blends with the clag to make the run essentially blind, visibility literally just a couple of feet. At times like these, the accumulated experience of those previous ascents is invaluable. We always say that we recognise every rock, that we can distinguish distinctive clumps of grass; that we could, if forced at gunpoint, do it blindfold.

The Collie reflects its location – not far from the border, but equally accessible from the rural hinterland and hill villages, you will hear both Welsh and English spoken throughout the pub. Further west, of course, our mountain races take place in the culturally distinctive heartland of Welsh speaking culture; with the events often serving to advertise that fact to the broader community of mountain runners who sometimes come from across the UK to test themselves against some of our better known races.

Ras y Moelwyn, which styles itself 'the best fell race in Britain', is a case in point. It has twice hosted the British Championships in recent years, attracting the elite of the sport from the top clubs in the Lakes, Peak, Scotland, Isle of Man and Ireland. In 2019, it started from the centre of that most distinctive of Welsh towns, making a deliberate and admirable attempt to emphasise Blaenau's quarrying heritage. Hundreds of runners gathered in Rawson Square opposite the old Ty Gorsaf hotel: all looking up with some trepidation to the peaks of the Moelwynion range, anticipating the imminent physical distress of running up them: from this vantage point in the middle of town, all three of them (four if you count Craigysgafn) loom above the tottering heaps of slate that make Blaenau so unique. The experience left a lasting impression on many of the English raiders, as did the race itself, with the mist descending just as we emerged from Cwm Croesor onto the lower slopes of Moelwyn Mawr, swallowing up the big field instantly, and helping canny locals nip across advantageous short-cuts away from the prying eyes of the visiting athletes, some of whom were legends of the sport.

1. A winter morning on Bryn Alyn; 2. Another classic running traverse: the Rhinogydd from Barmouth to Trawsfynydd. Most runners slow considerably when they reach the notorious northern end pictured here, without doubt the most arduous terrain in Wales.

Jeremy Rifkin, in his *Age of Access*, attempted to define and trace the boundaries of late stage capitalism. We have all the white goods, technological gadgets and consumer durables we can ever need, so what is left to sell? The answer is obvious: life itself, the commodification of human experience. We are now continually exhorted to seek new experiences, not things, and we are told to complete our 'bucket list' before it is too late. Music festivals and important football matches sell out in a few minutes, as do big ticket road races and, increasingly, mountain races. Some would call this 'hypercapitalism' in the sense that we may think we have escaped the trap by avoiding shopping malls and the acquisition of stuff, but we are still consuming, still hooked into the tentacles of the system.

Fell races, at their best, resist all of this. They are defined by their unwillingness to join in the charade. They are not 'tough mudders' or expensive ultra-marathons: they are a few quid to enter. Nobody makes any money, nobody boasts about their achievements. And the inherent freedom of simply running in the hills, unencumbered, unrecorded by devices, can never be taken away from those that want, and need, to continue to reap its mental and physical rewards.

But there are a multitude of threats from all sides. Midweek races that are run largely for profit, 'trail races' that mirror big city marathons in their pricing structure, even short races in the hills that charge six or seven times the entry fee of a traditional fell race but cover the same terrain and target runners who may be entirely unaware of the ethos and traditions of British mountain running – whilst also deliberately dramatizing the nature of the event. It is analogous to developments in other outdoor sports, many of which will be familiar to many fell runners (given the interconnected Venn diagram that exists between us) whereby, for example, climbing walls and bolted sports climbing coexist alongside traditionally protected routes on Snowdonian crags. There might be space for the £4 entry on the day grassroots event to survive alongside the technical t-shirt commercial alternative. On the other hand, there might not.

Craig Jones, the chair of the Welsh Fell Runners Association, remains a staunch upholder of the fundamental tenets of fell running: 'My views on the sport are passionate, and fairly well known. I recently heard that a certain local commercial organiser who I know doesn't like me, and who was speaking in polite company, referred to me as a "traditionalist", which made me smile. I'm happy to accept that handle.' This view from the top of the sport filters down, it has an impact on those new to it that may themselves have come from a more commercial sporting background, where they may have become accustomed to those norms. And once given a basic grounding in the principles of fell running, most thinking people – whatever their own political persuasion – can appreciate the inherent nobility of a sport that remains free from the dirty hand of commerce. There is a reason that the sport refuses to compromise, that those principles should be conveyed as something akin to a holy writ.

The obvious contemporary question is whether the younger generation, notable by their absence at many races[9], values the lack of commerciality, or even recognises it. How should one boast on social media about a race or sport that nobody has heard of, with a downbeat, purely descriptive title? How to quantify the 'achievement'? The tradition of downplaying, of modesty, of the low key, might not survive the generational transition.

But there are grounds for optimism. With thousands of young people keenly aware of environmental issues and the importance of finding local solutions to global problems, many seem certain to seek sustainability in their sports and leisure activities. Rifkin offered a partial solution to the problem he diagnosed, suggesting that emphasising the regional and the distinctive might offer a way out of what he called the hypercapitalist conundrum: arguing that social movements underscore the local and historical and cannot be appropriated for profit. Could there be a better example of 'social movements underscoring the local' than Welsh fell running?

The glory of traditional mountain running is that it does not shout from the rooftops, it doesn't seek to convert, it doesn't make a song and dance about achievements or celebrate them on social media or Strava. It is gloriously pointless – it doesn't mean anything at all. Unless you have an ego – and there are not too many of those in traditional fell running – it is allowed to speak for itself. One of the reasons for this is that measurements of 'success', as with all forms of running, can only ever be relative. Any fell runner is aware that his or her own achievements pale into insignificance besides those of the legends of the sport: running is so quantifiable that it has a tendency to mitigate against ego. Unlike other sports, there is nowhere to hide.

Even the keenest enthusiasts tend not to be evangelists for the sport, preferring to keep things low key, recognising the fragility of the landscape and the sport itself. That does not make it exclusive, merely cautious.

1. *Yr Elen on the old Carneddau race route;*
2. *Yr Elen;*
3. *Descending Pen yr Helgi Du on the Porthmadog-Conwy 'Sea to Sea'.*

[9] I remember a round of applause a few years ago at the start-line of the Stretton Skyline race, just across the border in Shropshire, to show appreciation for the unusual sight of a handful of under 30-year-olds that had turned up to compete in that long and hard event over the region's surprisingly steep hills. In recent years, there has been a small but noticeable influx of younger runners, however, which bodes well for the future.

There is something of the ancient 'art' versus 'science' dichotomy about this. Fell running is an art, not a science. Whereas the increasingly common phenomenon (often seen in ultra marathons) of downloading a route and then following it, heads down, looking at a line on your watch, is *definitely* a science. The organisers of big, profit-orientated off-road events now tend to require runners to do precisely this. From their point of view, you can see the appeal. No need for marshalls, no need to mark the course, just depend on the technology and rake in the profits.

I've done events like this on numerous occasions, and for me (not remotely technically minded) it took years for the penny to drop as I watched my competitors following that GPS line while I struggled with inadequate OS maps. But it all lacks nuance, it lacks charm, and it is also dangerous – as mountain rescue teams across Britain will attest, with numerous examples of walkers and runners lost on the hills as their batteries expire. So the ruling fell running bodies, very wisely, now ban the use of GPS devices on traditional fell races, correctly reasoning that they encourage the wrong sorts of people to enter the wrong kinds of events, and potentially lure runners into a dangerously false sense of security. Instead, a map and compass is required, in time-honoured fashion – and art chalks up a rare win against science.

'Art' can of course be taken too far in the battle with science. French situationists and psychogeographers used to argue that maps divorced people from the world they inhabited, and encouraged them to think they lived in a virtual environment, reducing its topography to a series of coordinates and contours. No serious fell runner or mountain athlete would go that far, because knowing precisely where we are is an essential part of remaining safe in our favourite environment. But the rise of GPS,

Strava and Smartphones is pertinent here – the conceit of feeling in control of the landscape is misplaced and potentially dangerous, and detracts from the essential experience of 'being' in the landscape.

That sense of complete immersion into the mountain landscape is perhaps the thing we mountain runners should value most. For the psychogeographers, going off the map was a way of reclaiming the world. For us, clinging on to the fundamental principles of the map and compass is a way of retaining those basic principles of hillcraft and self-sufficiency.

The sense of liberation that running in the hills can provide cannot be properly compared to anything else. There is something about its lightness of touch, its essential purity and bond with the landscape, that other mountain sports – encumbered with expensive, unwieldy equipment – cannot hope to match. And when you are properly racing, brain starved of oxygen, entering a particular state of mental oblivion familiar to all fell runners, that most modern of clichés – mindfulness – is truly apposite. You have to live in the moment, because your world shrinks to the ground beneath your feet, past and future dissolve, leaving only the present.

The races described in this book, while fundamentally competitive, all conform to those basic fell running principles. None of them is run for profit. All of them encourage self-sufficiency in the mountains and celebrate the primeval joy of *treading lightly* through the spectacular, challenging landscapes of upland Wales. All of them cleave to the central principle of sustainability, and have done so for decades, long before such notions entered the global political lexicon. For the time being at least, fell running remains a haven from commercialism and an expression of the authentic in an increasingly inauthentic world.

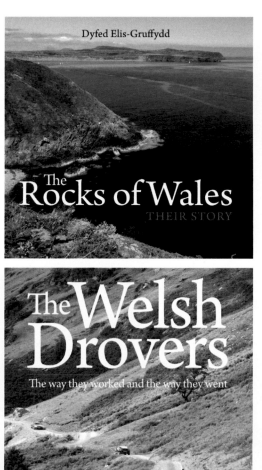
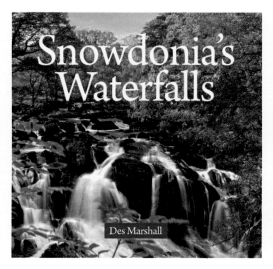

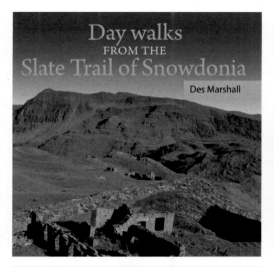

Day walks
FROM THE
Slate Trail of Snowdonia

Des Marshall

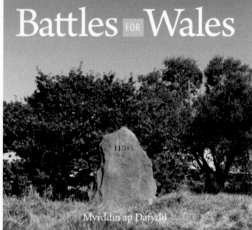

Battles FOR Wales

Myrddin ap Dafydd

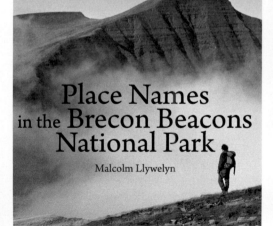

Place Names
in the Brecon Beacons
National Park

Malcolm Llywelyn

The
Mountain Lakes
of Snowdonia

Des Marshall